Joseph Rodman Drake, Fitz-Greene Halleck

The Croakers

Joseph Rodman Drake, Fitz-Greene Halleck

The Croakers

ISBN/EAN: 9783743337022

Manufactured in Europe, USA, Canada, Australia, Japa

Cover: Foto ©ninafisch / pixelio.de

Manufactured and distributed by brebook publishing software (www.brebook.com)

Joseph Rodman Drake, Fitz-Greene Halleck

The Croakers

Bradford Club Series.

NUMBER TWO.

THE CROAKERS

BY

JOSEPH RODMAN DRAKE

AND

FITZ GREENE HALLECK

First Complete Edition

NEW YORK
MDCCCLX

Entered according to Act of Congress, in the year 1860,
by John B. Moreau,

FOR THE BRADFORD CLUB,

in the Clerk's Office of the District Court of the United States
for the Southern District of New York.

ONE HUNDRED COPIES PRINTED.

CLUB COPY.

PREFACE.

The publication, or rather, the printing a limited edition for private circulation, by special subscription, of the following poems, has arisen from the desire frequently expressed by the friends of the authors to possess the CROAKERS in an authentic form. More than once since their first appearance in the columns of the daily newspapers, efforts have been made for their collection in print, and one or two unauthorized gatherings have thus been made, while numerous copies more or less complete, prepared with considerable trouble, have been circulated in manuscript. There appears to be now a good opportunity for a more permanent edition of the poems. The times are sufficiently removed from the first publication to do away with any feeling of asperity, however slight, which may have attended their original appearance; for the verses occasionally, it must be admitted, had their sharp satirical points, though they were sheathed in good humor and alleviated by polished musical expression. While any feeling of hostility is thus obliterated, we are not too far removed from the date of these productions to lose the benefit of consultation with contemporaries in the explanation of allusions growing day by day more obscure. A liberal supply of notes, indeed, is indispensable to the understanding and enjoyment of the CROAKERS. These have been supplied with no little painstaking from the best resources at hand, and it is believed will present a fair claim to accuracy.

The collection will be found to contain several original Croakers by Mr. Halleck, which, though written at the period of the others, have not hitherto seen the light, while several additions of a similar nature have been made from the manuscripts of Drake. The new poems are indicated in the table of contents, to which we may also refer for the dates of publication.

We cannot present these youthful publications of the authors to the reader, without a farther expression of admiration, not merely of their felicity in literary execution which ranks them with the best local satires, but of the general good humor without harshness or ill will by which they are characterized. True wit and humor know how to gain their ends without lacerating the sensibilities of the individual. We are none of us out of the reach of these weapons, or insensible to their severities; but we believe it may be said of the CROAKERS, that their stroke, though never pointless, has inflicted no unseemly injury nor left any lasting wound. They are written in the language of poets with the self-respect of the gentleman. There are no lines to crop for their indelicacy, or apologies to be made for transgressing the privileged limits of this species of literature.

To New Yorkers, the CROAKERS will always have a special interest for their illustrations of the notable acts of notable men of the last generation in the city and state, and it may not be too much to say that what is in this way of real interest to New York, may not be altogether unworthy of attention in an historical point of view throughout the country.

CONTENTS.

		PAGE.
To Ennui,	Eve. Post, 10 March, '19,	1
On Presenting the Freedom of the City,	" 11 "	3
The Secret Mine,	" 12 "	5
When Bony Fought his Hosts of Foes,	Nat. Adv., 11 "	7
To Mr. Potter,	Eve. Post, 13 "	10
To Mr. Simpson,	" 15 "	12
The National Painting,	Nat. Adv., 15 "	14
The Battery War,	Eve. Post, 15 "	15
To Croaker Junior,	" 16 "	18
To De Witt Clinton,	" 16 "	20
To the Surgeon-General of New York,	" 17 "	23
To John Minshull,	" 18 "	25
The Man who Frets at Worldly Strife,	" 19 "	27
To E. Simpson, Esq.,	" 20 "	29
To John Lang, Esq.,	" 23 "	31
To Domestic Peace,	" 24 "	33
To E. Simpson, Esq.,	" 25 "	35
A Lament for Great Ones Departed,	" 27 "	37
To Captain Seaman Weeks,	" 8 April, '19,	40
Abstract of the Surgeon-Gen. Report,	" 10 "	42
To an Elderly Coquette,	" 15 "	45
To —— Esquire,	" 16 "	47
Ode to Impudence,	" 17 "	49
To Mrs. Barnes,	Nat. Adv., 19 "	51
To Simon,	Eve. Post, 20 "	54
A Loving Epistle to Mr. Wm. Cobbett,	" 1 May, '19,	57
The American Flag,	" 29 "	59

CONTENTS.

		PAGE.
The Forums,	Eve. Post, 4 June, '17,	62
Ode to Fortune,	" 9 "	65
The Love of Notoriety,	" 15 "	67
To Simeon De Witt, Esq.,	" 17 "	69
To E. Simpson, Esq.,	" 20 "	73
To * * * * *,	" 7 July, '19,	77
The Council of Appointment,	" 19 "	79
Curtain Conversations,	" 24 "	82
An Address for the Opening of the New Theatre,	" 21 Aug't, '21,	84
To Walter Bowne, Esq.,	N. Y. Mir., 26 Jan'y, '28,	87
The Recorder,	Eve. Post, - -	91
To Robert Hogbin,	" 16 Nov'r, '30,	104
The Dinner Party,	Home Jour. 27 May, '56,	107
The Tea Party,	" 27 "	110
The Modern Hydra,	unpublished, - -	112
The Meeting of the Grocers,	" - -	114
The King of the Doctors,	" - -	116
Mr. Clinton's Speech, Jan. 1825,	" - -	118
The Nightmare,	" - -	122
To the Directors of the Acad. of Arts,	" - -	124
Oh! where are now the Lights that Shed,	" - -	127
To Quackery,	" - -	129
The Militia,	" - -	132

THE CROAKERS.

TO ENNUI.

Avaunt! arch enemy of fun,
   Grim nightmare of the mind:
Which way great Momus! shall I run,
   A refuge safe to find?
My puppy's dead—Miss Rumor's breath
   Is stopt for lack of news,
And Fitz is almost hyp'd to death,
   And Lang[1] has got the blues.

I've read friend Noah's[2] book quite thro'
   Appendix, notes and all;
I've swallowed Lady Morgan's[3] too,
   And blundered through De Stael:
The Edinburg Review—I've seen't
   The last that has been shipt;
I've read—in short—all books in print,
   And some in manuscript.

I'm sick of General Jackson's toast,
   Canals are nought to me:
Nor do I care who rules the roast
   Clinton—or John Targee:
No stock in any Bank I own,
   I fear no Lottery shark
And if the Battery were gone,
   I'd ramble in the Park.

Let gilded Guardsmen shake their toes,
   Let Altorf[4] please the pit,
Let Mister Hawkins[5] "blow his nose"
   And Spooner[6] publish it:
Insolvent laws let Marshall[7] break,
   Let dying Baldwin[8] cavil;
And let tenth ward electors shake
   Committees to the devil.

In vain—for like a cruel cat
   That sucks a child to death,
Or like a Madagascar bat,
   Who poisons with his breath,
The fiend—the fiend is on me still;
   Come, doctor!—here's your pay—
What lotion, potion, plaster, pill,
   Will drive the beast away?

                               CROAKER.

ON PRESENTING[9]

THE FREEDOM OF THE CITY

IN A GOLD BOX TO A GREAT GENERAL.

The board is met—the names are read;
   Elate of heart, the glad committee
Declare the mighty man has said
   He'll take "the freedom of the city."
He thanks the council, and the mayor,
   Presents 'em all, his humble service;
And thinks he's time enough to spare
   To sit an hour or so with Jarvis.

Hurra! hurra! prepare the room—
   Skaats![10] are the ham and oysters come?
Go—make some savoury whiskey punch,
   The General takes it with his lunch;
For a sick stomach, 'tis a cure fit
   And vastly useful in a surfeit.

But see! the mayor is in the chair,
    The council is convened again;
And ranged in many a circle fair,
    The ladies and the gentlemen
Sit mincing, bowing, smiling, talking
    Of congress—balls—the Indian force—
Some think the General will be walking,
    And some suppose he'll ride of course:
And some are whistling—some are humming—
    And some are peering in the Park
To try if they can see him coming;
    And some are half asleep—when hark!

A triumph on the war-like drum,
    A heart-uplifting bugle strain,
A fife's far flourish—and "they come!"
    Rung from the gathered train.
Sit down—the fun will soon commence—
    Quick! quick your honour! mount your place;
Present your loaded compliments,
    And fire a volley in his face.

They're at it now—great guns and small—
    Squib, cracker, cannon, musquetry;
Dear General! though you swallow all;
    I must confess it sickens me.

                        CROAKER.

THE "SECRET" MINE"

SPRUNG AT A LATE SUPPER.

The songs were good, for Mead[12] and Hawkins sung 'em,
   The wine went round, 'twas laughter all, and joke;
When crack! the General sprung *a mine* among 'em,
   And beat a safe retreat amid the smoke:
As fall the sticks of rockets, when we fire 'em,
   So fell the Bucktails at that toast accurst;
Looking like Korah, Dathan and Abiram,
   When the firm earth beneath their footsteps burst.

Quell'd is big Haff[13] who oft has fire and flood stood,
   More pallid grows the snowy cheek of Rose,
Cold sweats bedew the leathern hide of Bloodgood,[14]
   Deep sinks the concave of huge Edwards' nose.
But see the Generals Colden[15] and Bogardus,[16]
   Joy sits enthroned in each elated eye;
While Doyle[17] and Mumford[18] clap their fists as hard as
   The iron mauls in Pierson's factory.

The midnight conclave met, good Johnny Targee
    Begins (as usual) to bestow advice;
"Declare the General a fool, I charge ye!
    And swear the toast was not his own free choice;
Tell 'em that Colden prompted—and maintain it.
    That is the fact, I'm sure; but we can see
By sending Aleck down to ascertain it."
    That hint was taken, and accordingly

A certain member had a conversation
    And asked a certain surgeon all about it;
Some folks assert he got the information;
    'Tis also said, he came away without it:
Good people all! I'm up to more than you know;
    But prudence frowns—my coward goose quill lingers,
For fear that flint and trigger, Doctor[19] Bronaugh
    Should slip a challenge in your poet's fingers!

                                        CROAKER.

"*There was captain Cucumber, lieutenant Tripe, ensign Pattypan, and myself.*"

Mayor of Garratt.

When Bony fought his hosts of foes,
Heroes and generals arose
   Like mushrooms when he bade them:
Europe, while trembling at his nod,
Thought him a sort of demi-god—
   So wondrous quick he made them.

But every dog must have his day;
Poor Bony's power has passed away;
   His track let others follow.
Yet in the talent of the great,
With dash of goose quill to create,
   Our Clinton[20] beats him hollow!

Alas! thou little god[21] of war,
The proud effulgence of thy star
   Is dimmed, I fear, for ever;
Though bright thy buttons long have shined,
And still thy powdered hair behind,
   Is clubbed so neat and clever.

Yet round thee are assembled now
New chieftains, all intent as thou
   On hard militia duty:—
There's King[23] conspicuous for his hat,
And Ferris Pell[24] for God knows what—
   And Bayard,[25] for his beauty.

These are but colonels—there are hosts
Of higher grades, like Banquo's ghosts
   Upon my sight advancing,
In truth, they made e'en Jackson stare.
When in the Park, uptossed in air,
   He saw their plumage dancing.

Yet I should wrong them not to name
Two major-generals, high in fame—
   By Heaven! a gallant pair!
(They haven't any soldiers yet)
His honour, *general* by brevet,
   Bogardus—*brevet* mayor.

THE CROAKERS.

Should England dare to send again
Her scoundrel red coats o'er the main,
   I fear some sad disaster:
Each soldier wears an epaulette;
The Guards have turned a capering set,
   And want a dancing master.

Sam Swartwout,[26] where are now your Grays?
Oh! bid again their banner blaze
   O'er hearts and ranks unbroken:—
Let drum and fife your slumbers break,
And bid the Devil freely take
   Your meadows at Hoboken.

                     CROAKER, JUNIOR.

TO MR. POTTER,[7]

THE VENTRILOQUIST.

Dear Sir:

You've heard that Mr. Robbin[28]
   Has brought in, without rhyme or reason,
A bill to send you jugglers hopping;
   That bill will pass this very season:
Now as you lose your occupation,
   And may perhaps be low in coffer,
I send for your consideration
   The following very liberal offer.

Five hundred down, by way of bounty,
   Expenses paid, (as shall be stated)
Next April to Chenango county;
   And there we'll have you nominated:
Your duty 'll be, to watch the tongues
   When Root's[29] brigade begins to skirmish,
To stop their speeches in their lungs,
   And bring out such as I shall furnish.

Thy ventriloquial powers, my Potter!
  Shall turn to music every word,
And make the Martling[30] deists utter
  Harmonious anthems to our Lord.
Then, all their former tricks upsetting,
  To honey thou shalt change their gall,
For Sharpe[31] shall vindicate brevetting,
  And Root admire the great canal.

It will be pleasant too, to hear a
  Decent speech among our swains;
We almost had begun to fear a
  Famine for the dearth of brains:
No more their tongues shall play the devil,
  Thy potent art the fault prevents;
Now German[32] shall, for once be civil,
  And Bacon[33] speak with common sense.

Poor German's head is but a leaker;
  Should yours be found compact and close.
As you're to be the only speaker,
  We'll make you speaker of the house—
If you're in haste to "touch the siller,"
  Dispatch me your acceptance merely,
And call on trusty Mr. Miller,[34]
  He'll pay the cash—
            Sir,
              Yours, sincerely,
                CROAKER.

TO MR. SIMPSON,[35]

MANAGER OF THE THEATRE.

I'm a friend to your theatre, oft have I told you,
    And a still warmer friend, Mr. Simpson, to you,
And it gives me great pain, be assured, to behold you
    Go fast to the devil, as lately you do.
We scarcely should know you were still in existence,
    Were it not for the play bills one sees in Broadway;
The newspapers all seem to keep at a distance;
    Have your puffers deserted for want of their pay?

Poor Woodworth![36] his Chronicle died broken hearted;
    What a loss to the drama! the world and the age!
And Coleman[37] is silent since Philipps departed,
    And Noah's too busy to think of the stage.
Now, the aim of this letter is merely to mention
    That since all your critics are laid on the shelf,
Out of pure love to you, it is my kind intention
    To take box No. 3, and turn critic myself.

Your ladies are safe — if you please you may say it,
  Perhaps they have faults — but I'll let them alone;
Yet I owe two a debt — 'tis my duty to pay it,
  Of them I must speak in a kind, friendly tone.
Mrs. Barnes — Shakspeare's heart would have beat had
    he seen her;
  Her magic has drawn from me many a tear,
And ne'er shall my pen or its satire chagrin her,
  While pathos and genius and feeling are dear.

And there's sweet Miss Leesugg,[38] by the bye, she's not
    pretty,
  She's a little too large, and has not too much grace,
Yet there is something about her so witching and witty,
  'Tis pleasure to gaze on her good humoured face.
But as for your men — I don't mean to be surly —
  They soon may expect to have each one his due;
For the present — there's Olliff's a famous Lord Bur-
    leigh.
  And Hopper[39] and Maywood[40] are promising too.

              Yours,

                        CROAKER, JUNIOR.

THE NATIONAL PAINTING.[a]

Awake! ye forms of verse divine—
   Painting! descend on canvass wing,
And hover o'er my head Design!
   Your son, your glorious son I sing!
At Trumbull's[b] name, I break my sloth,
   To load him with poetic riches;
The Titian of a table cloth!
   The Guido of a pair of breeches!

Come star-eyed maid—Equality!
   In thine adorer's praise I revel;
Who brings, so fierce his love to thee—
   All forms and faces to a level:
Old, young—great, small—the grave, the gay;
   Each man might swear the next his brother,
And there they stand in dread array,
   To fire their votes at one another.

How bright their buttons shine! how straight
　　Their coat-flaps fall in plaited grace;
How smooth the hair on every pate;
　　How vacant each immortal face!
And then thy tints—the shade—the flush—
　　(I wrong them with a strain too humble)
Not mighty Sherred's[13] strength of brush
　　Can match thy glowing hues, my Trumbull.

Go on, great painter! dare be dull;
　　No longer after nature dangle;
Call rectilinear beautiful;
　　Find grace and freedom in an angle:
Pour on the red—the green—the yellow—
　　" Paint 'till a horse may mire upon it,"
And while I've strength to write or bellow,
　　I'll sound your praises in a sonnet.

　　　　　　　　　　　　CROAKER.

THE BATTERY WAR.*

" Twice twenty shoe-boys, twice two dozen guards.
Chairman and porters — hackney coachmen — Dandies!"
Tom Thumb.

"Here Dickens!—Go fetch my great coat and umbrella,
   Tell Johnny and Robert to put on their shoes;
And Dickens— take something to drink, my good fellow,
   You may go with Tom Ostler, along, if you choose:
You must put your new coat on — but mind, and be quiet
   Till my clerk, Mr. Scribble, shall tip you the wink,
Then roar like the devil — hiss — kick up a riot!
   I imagine we'll settle the thing in a twink."

Arrived at the Hall[45] they were nothing too early:
   Little Hartman[46] was placed, like king log, in the chair,
Supported, for contrast, by modest king Charley;
   The general was speaking, who is to be mayor:
Undaunted, he stood in the midst of the bobberie,
   Clerks — footmen — and Dandies — ye gods! what a noise.
No thief in Fly-Market, just caught in a robbery,
   Could raise such a clatter of blackguards and boys.

Mercein[7] and Bogardus each told a long story,
   Very fine without doubt to such folks as could hear;
Then the two kings resigned, and in high gig and glory,
   The light-footed chief of the guards took the chair,
So he made them a speech, about little or nothing,
   Except he advised 'em "to go home to bed;"
And the simple fact is, that, in spite of their mouthing,
   'Twas the only good, sensible, thing that was said.

Bye the way, though — we've heard that these sons of
      sedition,
   These "vile Bonapartes," (to quote Jemmy Lent,)[8]
Are about to bring forward a second edition,
   And Squire McGarraghan "fears the event."
Now, to let our wise council their honest game play
      on yet,
   Just call out, your honour, the Gingerbread Guards—
Bid them drive at the traitors with cutlass and bayonet,
   And then pick their pockets as bare—as your bards'.
                              CROAKER & CO.

TO CROAKER, JUNIOR.

Your hand, my dear Junior! we're all in a flame
   To see a few more of your flashes;
The Croakers for ever! I'm proud of the name —
But brother, I fear, though our cause is the same,
   We shall quarrel like Brutus and Cassius.

But why should we do so! 'tis false what they tell,
   That poets can never be cronies;
Unbuckle your harness, in peace let us dwell;
Our goose quills will canter together as well
   As a pair of Prime's[19] mouse color'd ponies.

Once blended in spirit, we'll make our appeal,
   And by law be incorporate too;
Apply for a charter in crackers to deal,
A fly-flapper rampant shall shine on our seal,
   And the firm shall be "Croaker & Co."

Fun! prosper the union — smile, fate, on its birth;
　　Miss Atropos shut up your scissors;
Together we'll range thro' the regions of mirth,
A pair of bright Gemini dropt on the earth,
　　The Castor and Pollux of quizzers.

CROAKER.

Mr. Editor—I wish you to precede the lines I send you enclosed, by republishing Mr. Hamilton's late letter to the governor *verbatim et literatim*, in order that the world may see, that on this occasion, at least, the poet does not deal in fiction.

"*To De Witt Clinton, governor of the State of New York:*"

"Sir—To your shame and confusion let it be recorded, that you dared not assume the responsibility of preserving to our national councils a patriotic and distinguished statesman, while you could advocate the publication of an insidious and base attack upon private character through the public organ of your administration. You know the motive of my visit to Mr. Root—you were not ignorant that the senatorial reëlection of Rufus King, was to me a subject of deep personal concern; and on this occasion you declared, that you had marked my course, and that this support should recoil with vengeance upon the republican party. To those intimate with your pusillanimity and intrigues, you disappoint no expectation. The traducer of America's brightest ornaments can only be consistent within the sphere of his degeneracy. It is the pride of the name I bear, to be distinguished by your envenomed malignity—one and all, we are opposed to your administration and your character. I am induced to make this explanation as a permanent obligation to the public; to my own feelings it is perfectly humiliating. I have the honour to remain your obedient servant,

ALEXANDER HAMILTON.

Assembly Chamber, March 8th, 1819.

A VERY MODEST LETTER

FROM ONE GREAT MAN TO ANOTHER.

"To be a well-favoured man is the gift of fortune, but to write and read comes by nature."—Dogberry.

How dare you, sir, presume to say
　　And write and print the paltry thing,
That I did wrong the other day,
　　To give my vote for Rufus King!

'Twas natural that I should take a
　　Particular interest in it, sir,
For I've been agent at Jamaica,[54]
　　And he a foreign minister.

You say, you've "*marked my course*" of late,
　　And mean to make what I've been doing
A means of breaking up the state,
　　And bringing on our party's ruin.

With all who've known your scoundrel tricks,
    Since first you came to curse the nation,
The Lucifer of politics!
    "*You disappoint no expectation.*"

It suits your mean and grovelling spirit
    Thus to attack great men like me;
You slander only chiefs of merit,
    Stars in our country's galaxy!

Elijah, when his task was done,
    His mantle o'er Elisha threw;
Now I'm my father's eldest son,
    And heir to all his talents too.

We're proud to say — the world well knows
    You never liked our family;
We "*one and all*" have been your foes,
    My brother Jim, and John and I.

For my own sake, you well may wonder
    That I these lines to you have sent,
It is to lay the public under
    An "*obligation permanent.*"

Assembly Chamber, March 8.

            Done into English verse by

                      CROAKER & Co.

TO THE SURGEON GENERAL[54]

OF THE STATE OF NEW YORK.

"*Why, Tom, he knows all things — An' it be not the devil himself, we may thank God,*"—Village Wizard.

Oh! Mitchill, lord of granite flints,
   Doctus, in law -- and wholesome dishes ;
Protector of the patent splints,
   The foe of whales — the friend of fishes ;
" Tom-Codus "—" Septon "—" Phlogobombos ! "[55]
   What title shall we find to fit ye ?
Inquisitor of sprats and compost !
   Or Surgeon General of Militia !

We hail thee !—mammoth of the state !
   Steam frigate ! on the waves of physic —
Equal in practice or debate,
   To cure the nation or the phthisic :
The amateur of Tartar dogs !
   Wheat-flies, and maggots that create 'em !
Of mummies ! and of mummy-chogs ![56]
   Of brick-bats — lotteries — and pomatum !

It matters not how low or high it is,
    Thou knowest each hill and vale of knowledge;
Fellow of forty-nine societies!
    And lecturer in David's College —
And when thou diest — (for life is brief;)
    Thy name, in all its gathered glory,
Shall shine, immortal! as the leaf
    Of Delaplaine's Repository.[56]

CROAKER & Co.

TO JOHN MINSHULL, ESQ.[57]

POET AND PLAYWRIGHT;

FORMERLY OF MAIDEN LANE, BUT NOW ABSENT IN EUROPE.

Oh! bard of the west, hasten back from Great Britain!
  Our harp-strings are silent, they droop on the tree;
What poet among us, is worthy to sit in
  The chair whose fair cushion was hallowed by thee?
In vain the wild clouds o'er our mountain-tops hover,
  Our rivers flow sadly, our groves are bereft;
They have lost—and forever! their poet, their lover!
  And Woodworth and Paulding are all we have left.

Great Woodworth, the champion of Buckets and Freedom,
  Thou "editor, author and critic" to boot,
I must leave thy rich volumes to those that can read 'em,
  For my part I never had patience to do 't.
And, as for poor Upham, (who in a fine huff says
  He'll yield to no Briton the laurel of wit,)
Alas! they have "stol'n his ideas," as Puff says,
  I had read all his poems before they were writ.

But hail! to thee Paulding,[58] the pride of the Backwood!
  The poet of cabbages, log huts and gin,
God forbid thou should'st get in the clutches of
    Blackwood,
  Oh Lord! how the wits of Old England would grin:
In pathos — Oh! who could be flatter or funnier?
  Were ever descriptions more vulgar and tame?
I wronged thee, by Heaven! when I said there were
    none here
  Could cope with great Minshull, thou peer of his
    fame!

CROAKER.

> "*A merry heart goes all the way,
> A sad one tires in a mile-a.*"
>
> Winter's Tale.

The man who frets at worldly strife
　Grows sallow, sour, and thin;
Give us the lad whose happy life
　Is one perpetual grin:
He, Midas like, turns all to gold,
　He smiles when others sigh,
Enjoys alike the hot and cold,
　And laughs thro' wet and dry.

There's fun in every thing we meet,
　The greatest, worst and best;
Existence is a merry treat,
　And every speech a jest:
Be't ours to watch the crowds that pass
　Where mirth's gay banner waves;
To show fools thro' a quizzing glass,
　And bastinade the knaves.

The serious world will scold and ban,
    In clamour loud and hard,
To hear Meigs[59] called a congressman,
    And Paulding styled a bard:
But come what may — the man's in luck
    Who turns it all to glee,
And laughing cries, with honest Puck,
    "Good Lord! what fools ye be."
CROAKER.

TO E. SIMPSON, ESQ.,[a]

ON WITNESSING THE REPRESENTATION OF THE NEW TRAGEDY OF BRUTUS.

I have been every night — whether empty or crowded,
   And taken my seat in your box No. 3,
In a sort of poetical Scotch mist I'm shrouded,
   As the far-fam'd Invisible Girl used to be.

As a critic professed, 'tis my province to flout you,
   And hiss as they did at poor Charley's Macheath,
But all is so right and so proper about you,
   That I'm forced to be civil — in spite of my teeth.

In your dresses and scenery, classic and clever!
   Such invention! such blending of old things and new!
Let Kemble's proud laurels be withered forever!
   Wear the wreath, my dear Simpson, 'tis fairly your due.

How "*apropos*" now was that street scene in Brutus,
   Where the sign "*Coffee-house*" in plain English was writ!
By the way, "*Billy Niblo's*" would much better suit us,
   And box, pit and gallery roar at the wit.

How sparkled the eyes of the raptured beholders,
　To see Kilner⁶¹ — a Roman — in robes "a-la-Gree!"
How graceful they flowed o'er his neatly-turned
　　shoulders!
　How completely they set off his Johnny Bull neck!

But to hint at the thousand fine things that amuse me
　Would take me a month — so adieu 'till my next.
And your actors — they must for the present excuse me;
　One word though, "*en-passant,*" for fear they'll be
　　vex'd:

Moreland,⁶² Howard⁶³ and Garner⁶⁴ — the last importa-
　tion!
　Three feathers, as bright as the Prince Regent's
　　plume!
Though puffing is, certainly, not my vocation,
　I always shall praise *them* — whenever I've room.

With manners — so formed to persuade and to win ye!
　With faces — one need but to look on to love!
Like Jefferson's Natural Bridge in Virginia —
　"*Worth a royage across the Atlantic,*" by Jove!!

　　　　　　　　　　　　CROAKER, JUNIOR.

TO JOHN LANG, ESQ.[65]

"And still they gaz'd, and still the wonder grew,
That one small head could carry all he knew."

Goldsmith.

We've twined the wreath of honor
   Round Doctor Mitchill's brow;
Though bold and daring was the theme,
   A loftier waits us now.
In thee — Immortal LANG![66] have all
   The Sister Graces met —
Thou Statesman! Sage! and "*Editor*"
   Of the New York Gazette!

A second Faustus in thine art!
   The Newton of our clime!
The Bonaparte of Bulletins![67]
   The Johnson of thy time! —
At thy dread name, the "*terriers*" bark,
   The "*rats*" fly to their holes!
Thou Prince of "*petty paragraphs!*"
   "*Red Notes,*" and "*Signal Poles!*"

There's genius in thy speaking face —
   There's greatness in thine air —
Take " *Franklin's bust* " from [68] off thy roof,
   And place thine own head there!
" *Eight corners within pistol shot* "
   Long with thy fame have rang!
And " *Blue-Birds* " sung — and " *mad-cows* " lowed
   The name of Johnny Lang!

                                    CROAKER & Co.

TO DOMESTIC PEACE.

"Malbrook s'en va-t-en guerre."

Oh! Peace! ascend again thy throne,
   Resume the spotless olive leaf!
Display thy snowy muslin gown,
And wave o'er this distracted town,
   Thy cambric pocket handkerchief!

Or, if thou dost not like the dress
   (We own we have our doubts upon it),
Come like some pretty Quakeress,
And let thine orbs of quietness
   Shine, dove-like, from a satin bonnet!

We need thee, row-abhorring maid!
   The dogs of party bark alarms,
And ere the Battery-tax is laid,
And ere the next election's made,
   E'en Murray's Guards will rush to arms.

Feds, Coodies,[69] Bucktails,[70] — all in flame —
  With peals of nonsense frighten thee;
Sweet Peace! thou wert not much to blame,
If thou shouldst loathe the very name
  Of Clinton, or of John Targee.

For us, enthron'd in elbow chair,
  Thy foes alone with ink we sprinkle;
We love to smooth the cheek of care,
Until we leave no furrow there,
  Save laughter's evanescent wrinkle.

With thee and Mirth, we'll quit the throng —
  Each hour shall see our pleasures vary;
Jarvis[71] shall bring his *Cats* along,
And Lynch[72] shall float in floods of song,
  Pure as his highest-priced Madeira!

CROAKER & CO.

TO E. SIMPSON, ESQ.,

MANAGER OF THE NEW YORK THEATRE.

Mr. Philipps[73] has gone — and he carries away with him
    Much of my cash — and my hearty good will:
To both he is welcome, and long may they stay with
    him —
    Poor as he's made me, I'll cherish him still.

For when the wild spell of his melody bound me,
    I marked not the flight of the gay, happy hours;
His music created a fairy land round me,
    Above it, was sunshine — below it, were flowers.

But 'tis folly to weep — we must cease to regret him —
    Look about — you have many as brilliant a star:
There's Barnes,[74] (you may laugh if you will,) but just
    let him
    Play Belino[75] for once; — he'll beat Philipps by far!

When he sings *Love's Young Dream*, every heart will
   be beating,
  The ladies shall wave their white kerchiefs in air;
And peals of applauses shall hail the repeating
  Of his *Eveleen's Bower*, and his *Robin Adair!*

Fancy's Sketch! such fine *shakes* and such comic
   expression
  He'll give it; — 'twill put all the fiddles in tone!
And let Olliff (clean-shaved, with a new hero dress on),
  Play Baron Toraldi "*for that night alone.*"

If you wish to give all your acquaintances delight, or
  Fill your house to the brim — take this hint — it
   will go;
The humour will make e'en your candles burn brighter,
  And crowd every seat — to the very fourth row.

Besides *entre-nous*, there's another good reason —
  Perhaps 'twill the proud heart of Beekman[76] beguile;
He *may* promise to lower the rent the next season,
  And, for once in his life, — take his hat off and smile.

CROAKER, JUNIOR.

A LAMENT FOR GREAT ONES DEPARTED.

"Hung be the Heavens with black."
  Shakspeare.

There is a gloom on every brow,
  A sadness in each face we see:
The City Hall is lonely now,
  The Franklin Bank[77] looks wearily!

The Surgeon's Hall[78] in Barclay street,
  Wears to the eye a ghastlier hue!
And Staten Island's *Summer-seat*
  Has lost its best attraction too!

Well may we mourn — a stage and four
  (Our curse upon the rogue that drove it!)
From out our City lately bore
  All that adorn — and grace, and love it,

Ah! little knew each scoundrel horse
  How much they vex'd, and griev'd, and marred us,
They cared not sixpence for the loss
  We feel in Colden and Bogardus.

And Doctor Mitchill, LL. D.,
    And Tompkins,[79] Lord of Staten Isle!
Hush'd be the strain of mirth and glee,
    'Twere treason now to laugh or smile.

Long has proud Albany, elate,
    Reared her two steeples [80] high in air,
And boasted that she ruled the state,
    Because the *Governor lives there!*

But loftier now will be her tone,
    To know — within her walls are met
The brightest gems that ever shone
    Upon a city's coronet.

Tho' heavy is our load of pain,
    To feel that fate has thus bereft us,
Some consolations yet remain,
    For Dickey Riker still is left us!

And Hope, with smile and gesture proud,
    Points to a day of triumph nigh,
When like a sunbeam from the cloud
    That dims, awhile, an April sky,

Our champions shall again return,
    Their pockets with new honours crowded;
Then every heart will cease to mourn,
    And hats no more in crape be shrouded.

The Park shall throng with merry feet,
  And boys and beauties hasten there,
To place the new Judge on his seat!
  And hail the great Bogardus, Mayor!

CROAKER & Co.

TO CAPTAIN SEAMAN WEEKS,

CHAIRMAN OF THE TENTH WARD INDEPENDENT ELECTORS.

Captain Weeks — your right hand — though I never
   have seen it,
  I shake it, on paper, full ten times a day.
I love your tenth ward, and I wish I lived in it;
  Do you know any house there to let against May?
I don't mind what the rent is, so long as I get off
  From these party-mad beings — these tongues without heads!
I'm asham'd to be seen, sir, among such a set of
  Clintonians, Tammanies,[81] Coodies, and Feds!

Besides, I'm nervous, and can't bear the racket
  These gentlemen make when they're begging for votes;
There's John Haff,[82] and Ben Bailey,[83] and Christian,[84] and Bracket,[85]
  Only think what fine music must come from *their* throats!
Colonel Warner[86] calls Clinton "*a star in the banner,*"
  Mapes[87] swears by his sword-knot he'll ruin us all!
While Meigs flashes out in his fine classic manner,
  "*The meteor gorgon of Clinton must fall!*"

In vain, I endeavor to give 'em a hint on
    Sense, reason, or temper — they laugh at it all :
For sense is nonsense, when it makes against Clinton,
    And reason is treason in Tammany Hall.[88]
So I mean (though I fear I shall seem unto some a
    Strange, obstinate, odd-headed kind of an elf)
To strike my old tent in the fourth, and become a
    " Tenth ward independent elector " myself.

                                    CROAKER.

ABSTRACT

OF THE SURGEON-GENERAL'S REPORT.

The Surgeon-General by *brevet*,
   With zeal for public service burning,
Thinks this a happy time to get
   Another chance to show his learning;
He has in consequence collected
   His wits — and stewed them in retorts;
By distillation thus perfected,
   He hopes to shine — and so *reports:*

That he has searched authorities
   From Johnson down to Ashe and Shelley,
And finds that a Militia is —
   What he is now about to tell ye;
Militia means — such citizens
   As e'en in peace are kept campaigning,
The gallant souls that shoulder guns!
   And twice a year go out a-training.

This point being fix'd, we must, I think, sir,
　Proceed unto the second part,—
Entitled Grog—a kind of drink, sir,
　Which by its action on the heart,
Makes men so brave, they dare attack
　A bastion at its angle salient;
This is a well-established fact—
　The very proverb says—*pot-valiant.*

Grog—I'll define it in a minute—
　Take gin, rum, whiskey or peach brandy,
Put but a little water in it,
　And that is Grog—now understand me,
I mean to say, that should the spirit
　Be left out by some careless dog—
It is—I wish the world may hear it!
　It is plain water, and not Grog.

Having precisely fix'd what Grog is,
　(My reas'ning, sir, that question settles!)
We next must ascertain what Prog is—
　Now Prog, in vulgar phrase, is victuals:
This will embrace all kinds of food,
　Which on the smoking board can charm ye,
And by digestion furnish blood;
　A thing essential in any army!

These things should all be swallowed warm,
　　For heat, digestion much facilitates ;
Cold is a tonic, and does harm ;
　　A tonic always, sir, debilitates.
My *plan* then is to raise, as fast
　　As possible, a *corps* of cooks,
And drill them daily from the last
　　Editions of my cookery books !

Done into English, and likewise into verse, by
Croaker & Co.

TO AN ELDERLY COQUETTE.

"Parcius junctas quatiunt fenestras."
Horace, Book 1, Ode 25.

Ah! Chloe![20] no more at each party and ball,
   You shine the gay queen of the hour;
The lip, that alluringly smiled upon all,
   Finds none to acknowledge its power:
No longer the hearts of the dandies you break,
   No poet adores you in numbers;
No billets-doux sweeten, nor serenades break,
   The peaceful repose of your slumbers.

Dissipation has clouded those eloquent eyes,
   That sparkled like gems of the ocean;
Thy bosom is fair — but its billowy rise
   Awakens no kindred commotion:
And pale are those rubies of rapture, where Love
   Had showered his sweetest of blisses;
And the wrinkles which time has implanted above,
   Are cover'd in vain with false tresses.

The autumn is on thee — fell scandal prepares
  To hasten the wane of thy glory:
Too soon disappointment will hand thee down stairs,
  And old maidenhood end the sad story:
For me — long escaped from your trammels — I choose
  To enlist in the new corps of jokers;
Abandoning Chloe, I kneel to the Muse,
  And, instead of love-ditties, write Croakers.

C.

TO —— ESQUIRE.

Come, shut up your Blackstone, and sparkle again
    The leader and light of our classical revels;
While statutes and cases bewilder your brain,
    No wonder you're vex'd, and beset with blue devils:
But a change in your diet will banish the blues;
    Then come, my old chum, to our banquet sublime;
Our wine shall be caught from the lips of the Muse,
    And each plate and tureen shall be delug'd in rhyme.

Scott, from old Albin, shall furnish the dishes
    With wild fowl and ven'son that none can surpass;
And Mitchill, who sung the amours of the fishes,
    Shall fetch his most exquisite tom-cod and bass.
Leigh Hunt shall select, at his Hampstead Parnassus,
    Fine *greens*, from the hot-bed, the table to cheer;
And Wordsworth shall carry whole bowls of molasses,
    Diluted with water from sweet Windermere.

To rouse the dull fancy, and give one an appetite,
  Black wormwood bitters Lord Byron shall bear;
And Montgomery bring (to consumptives a happy sight,)
  Tepid soup-meagre, and lean capillaire.
Coleman shall sparkle in old bottled cider,
  Roast-beef and potatoes friend Crabbe shall supply,
Rogers shall hash us an olla podrida,
  And the best of "*fat cabbage*" from Paulding we'll buy.

My Tennant — free, fanciful, laughing and lofty,
  Shall pour out tokay and Scotch whiskey like rain;
Southey shall sober our spirits with coffee,
  And Horace in London flash up in Champagne.
Tom Campbell shall cheer us with rosy Madeira,
  Refin'd by long-keeping — rich, sparkling, and pure,
And Moore, *pour chasse café*, to each one shall bear a
  Lip-witching bumper of *parfait amour*.

Then come to our banquet — Oh! how can you pause
  A moment between merry rhyme and dull reason?
Preferring the wit-blighting *Spirit of Laws*
  To the spirit of verse, is poetical treason!
Judge Phœbus will certainly issue his writ,
  No quirk or evasion your cause can make good, man;
Only think what you'll suffer, when sentenc'd to sit
  And be kept broad awake 'till you've read the Backwoodman.

                              CROAKER & Co.

ODE TO IMPUDENCE.

"*Integer vitæ, scelerisque purus.*"
Horace, Book I, Ode 22.

The man who wears a brazen face,
    Quite *a son aise*, his glass may quaff;
And whether in, or out of place,
    May twirl his stick, and laugh!
Useless to him the broad doubloon,
    Red note, or dollar of the mill;
Tho' all his gold be in the moon,
    His brass is current money still.
Thus — when my cash was at low water,
    At Niblo's[91] I sat down to dine;
And, after a tremendous slaughter
    Among the wild-fowl and the wine,
The *bill* before mine eyes was plac'd —
    When, slightly turning round my head,
"*Charge it*," cried I — the man amaz'd!
    Star'd — made his congee — and obey'd.

Oh! bear me to some forest thick,
    Where wampum'd Choctaws prowl alone;
Where ne'er was heard the name of *tick*,
    And *bankrupt* laws are quite unknown:
Or to some shop, by bucks abhorr'd,
    Where to the longing pauper's sorrow,
The curst inscription decks the board
    Of " *Pay to-day and trust to-morrow:*"
Or plunge me in the dungeon tower;
    With bolts and turnkeys blast mine eyes;
While, call'd from death by Marshall's power,
    The ghosts of murdered debts arise!
The easy dupes, I'll wheedle still,
    With looks of brass and words of honey;
And having scor'd a decent bill,
    Pay off my impudence for money.

CROAKER & CO.

TO MRS. BARNES.[92]

Dear Ma'am — We seldom take the pen
   To praise, for whim and jest our trade is;
We're used to deal with gentlemen,
To spatter folly's skirts, and then
   We're somewhat bashful with the ladies.

Nor is it meant to give advice;
   We dare not take so much upon us;
But merely wish, in phrase concise,
To beg you, Ma'am, and Mr. Price,[93]
   For God's sake, to have mercy on us.

Oh! wave again thy wand of power,
   No more in melo-dramas whine,
Nor toil Aladdin's lamp to scour,
Nor dance fandangoes by the hour
   To Morgiana's tambourine!

Think, lady, what we're doom'd to feel;
   By heaven! 'twould rouse the wrath of stoics
To see the queen of sorrows deal
In thundering, lofty — low, by Shiell,
   Or mad Mathurin's mock-heroics.

Away with passion's withering kiss;
   A purer spell be thine to win us;
Unlock the fount of holiness,
While gentle pity weeps in bliss,
   And hearts throb sweetly-sad within us.

Or call those smiles again to thee
   That shone upon the lip that wore them,
Like sun-drops on a summer sea
When waters ripple pleasantly
   To wanton winds that flutter o'er them.

When pity wears her willow wreath,
   Let Desdemona's woes be seen;
Sweet Beverly's confiding faith,
Or Juliet, loving on in death,
   Or uncomplaining Imogen.

When wit and mirth their temples bind,
   With thistle-shafts, o'erhung with flowers:
Then quaint and merry Rosalind,
Beatrice, with her April mind,
   And Dinah's simple heart be ours.

For long thy modest orb has been
    Eclipsed by heartless cold parade;
So sinks the light of evening's queen
When the dull earth intrudes between
    Her beauties from the sun to shade.

Let fashion's worthless plaudits rise
    At the deep tone, and practised start;[94]
Be thine, true feeling's stifled sighs,
Tears wrung from stern and stubborn eyes,
    And smiles, that sparkle from the heart.

CROAKER & Co.

A LICK AT A FASHIONABLE FOLLY

WHICH REIGNS AMONG THE SONS AND DAUGHTERS OF THE HIGHER ORDER, IN THE RENOWNED CITY OF GOTHAM, AT THIS PRESENT WRITING.

TO SIMON,[94]

THE COOK COMME IL FAUT.

Dear Simon! Prince of pastry cooks!
    Oysters, and ham, and cold neat's tongue!
Pupil of Mitchill's cookery books!
    And bosom friend of old and young!
Sure from higher, brighter sphere,
    In showers of gravy thou wert hurl'd;
To aid our routs and parties here,
    And grace the fashionable world!

Taught by thy art, we closely follow
    And ape the English lords and misses —
For music, we've the Black Apollo,
    And Mrs. Poppleton[96] — for kisses;
We borrow all the rest, you know;
    Our glass from Christie,[97] for the time,
Plate from our friends, to make a show,
    And cash, to pay small bills from Prime.

What tho' Old Squaretoes will not bless thee,
   He fears your power and dreads your bill;
Ma and the "pretty dears" caress thee,
   And pat thy cheek, and love thee still.
Oh Simon! how we envy thee!
   When belles, that long have frown'd on all,
Greet thee with smiles, and bend the knee,
   To beg you'll help them give a ball.

Though ungenteel it is to think,
   For thought affects the nerves and brain!
Yet oft we think of thee, and drink
   Thy health in Lynch's best champaigne:
'Tis pity that thy signal merit
   Should slumber in so low a station:
Act, Simon, like a lad of spirit,
   And thou, in time, may'st rule the nation.

Break up your Saturdays "*At home,*"
   Cut Guinea and your sable clan,
Buy a new eye-glass, and become
   A dandy and a gentleman:
You must speak French, and make a bow,
   Ten lessons are enough for that,
And Leavenworth will teach you how
   To wear your corsets and cravat!

Throw all your chambers into one,
 Hire fiddlers, glasses, barons[98] too,
And then invite the whole *haut-ton*,
 Ask Hosack, he can tell you who.
The great that are and wish to be,
 Within your brilliant rooms will meet,
And belles, of high and low degree,
 From Broadway up to Cherry street!

This will insure you free admission
 To all our routs for years to come,
And when you die, a long procession
 Of dandies shall surround your tomb.
We'll raise an *almond statue* where
 In dust your honoured head reposes,
Mothers shall lead their daughters there
 And bid them twine your bust with roses.

CROAKER & Co.

A LOVING EPISTLE

TO MR. WILLIAM COBBETT, OF NORTH HEMPSTEAD, LONG ISLAND.[99]

> *"Belov'd of Heaven! the smiling Muse shall shed*
> *Her moonlight halo on thy beauteous head!"*
>
> Campbell's Pleasures of Hope.

Pride, boast and glory of each hemisphere!
   Well known, and lov'd in both — great Cobbett, hail!
Hero of Botley there, and Hempstead here —
   Of Newgate, and a Pennsylvania jail.
Long shall this grateful nation bless the hour,
   When by the beadle and your debts pursu'd,
The victim, like fam'd Barrington,[100] of power,
   "*You left your country for your country's good!*"

Terror of Borough-mongers, Banks and Crowns!
   Thorburn the seedsman, and Lord Castlereagh!
Potato-tops fall withering at your frowns —
   Grand *Ruta Baga Turnip* of your day!
Banish the memory of the Lockhart's cane,
   And Philadelphia *pole-cats* from your mind;
Let the world scoff — still you and Hunt remain —
   Yourselves a host — the envy of mankind!

Whether, as once in *Peter Porcupine*,
    You curse the country, whose free air your breathe,
Or, as plain *William Cobbett* toil to twine
    Around your brows sedition's poison'd wreath,
Or, in your letter to Sir Francis,[101] tear
    All mortal ties asunder with your pen,
We trace you, gentle spirit, every where,
    And greet you, first of scribblers and of men.

Well may our hearts with pride and pleasure swell,
    To know that face to face we soon shall meet:
We'll gaze upon you as you stand and sell
    Grammars and *Garden Seeds* in Fulton street![102]
And praise your book that tells about the weather,
    "*Our laws, religion, hogs and things*" to boot,
Where your immortal talents teach together
    Turnips and "*young ideas how to shoot.*"

In recompense, that you've designed to make
    Choice of our soil above all other lands,
A purse we'll raise to pay your debts, and take
    Your unsold Registers off your hands.
For this we ask that you, for once, will show
    Some gratitude, and, if you can, be civil;
Burn all your books, sell all your pigs, and go —
    No matter where — to England, or the devil!!

                              CROAKER & CO.

THE AMERICAN FLAG.

When Freedom, from her mountain height,
   Unfurl'd her standard to the air,
She tore the azure robe of night,
   And set the stars of glory there!
She mingled with its gorgeous dyes
The milky baldric of the skies,
And striped its pure celestial white
With streakings of the morning light;
Then, from his mansion in the sun,
She call'd her eagle bearer down,
And gave into his mighty hand
The symbol of her chosen land!

Majestic monarch of the cloud!
   Who rear'st aloft thy regal form,
To hear the tempest-tramping loud,
And see the lightning-lances driven,
   When stride the warriors of the storm,
And rolls the thunder-drum of heaven!

Child of the Sun! to thee 'tis given
  To guard the banner of the free,
To hover in the sulphur smoke,
To ward away the battle stroke,
And bid its blendings shine afar,
Like rainbows on the cloud of war,
  The harbingers of victory!

Flag of the brave! thy folds shall fly,
The sign of hope and triumph high!
When speaks the signal trumpet-tone,
And the long line comes gleaming on,
(Ere yet the life-blood, warm and wet,
Has dim'd the glist'ning bayonet,)
Each soldier's eye shall brightly turn
To where thy meteor-glories burn,
And, as his springing steps advance,
Catch war and vengeance from the glance!
And when the cannon-mouthings loud,
Heave in wild wreaths the battle-shroud,
And gory sabres rise and fall,
Like shoots of flame on midnight's pall!
There shall thy victor-glances glow,
  And cowering foes shall sink beneath,
Each gallant arm that strikes below,
  The lovely messenger of death.

Flag of the seas! on ocean's wave
Thy star shall glitter o'er the brave,
When Death, careering on the gale,
Sweeps darkly round the bellied sail,
And frighted waves rush wildly back
Before the broad-sides reeling rack,
The dying wanderer of the sea
Shall look, at once, to heaven and thee,
And smile, to see thy splendours fly,
In triumph, o'er his closing eye.

Flag of the free heart's only home,
   By angel hands to valour given!
Thy stars have lit the welkin dome
   And all thy hues were born in heaven!
Forever float that standard sheet![101]
   Where breathes the foe but falls before us?
With Freedom's soil beneath our feet,
   And Freedom's banner streaming o'er us!

CROAKER & CO.

THE FORUMS.

"*You will recollect, gentlemen, your proper pauses, repetitions, hum's, ha's, and interjections — and you, the speaker, remember to be mighty dull — and you, the audience, to fall asleep!*"

Foote.

'Tis over — the fatal hour has come,
The voice of eloquence is dumb,
   Mute are the members of the Forum!
We've shed what tears we had to spare,
There now remains the pious care
   Of chaunting a sad requiem o'er 'em.

The Roman drank the Tyber's wave,
Ilissus' stream its virtues gave
   To bid the Grecian live forever;
Our Forum orators a draught
Of greater potency have quaff'd,
   Sparkling and pure from *the North River!*

Proudly our bosoms beat to claim
Communion with our country's fame,
At mention of each gallant name
   From Bunker's Hill to Chippewa!
All, who, on battle-field or wave,
Have met the death that waits the brave,
Or peal'd, above their foeman's grave,
   The victor's wild hurrah!

And he, who quell'd a tyrant king,
And "grasped the lightning's fiery wing,"
   Was nurtur'd in our country's bowers;
But now, a brighter gem is set
Upon her star-wrought coronet,
   The world's first orators are ours!

The name of every Forum chief[106]
Shall gleam upon our history's leaf,
   Circled with glory's fadeless fires;
And poet's pen and painter's pallet
Shall tell of William Paxson Hallett
   And Richard Varick Dey — Esquires!!

Resort of fashion, beauty, taste —
The Forum Hall was nightly grac'd
With all who blush'd their hours to waste
   At balls — and such ungodly places;
And Quaker girls were there allow'd
To show, among the motly crowd,
   Their sweet blue eyes and pretty faces.

And thither all our wise ones went,
On *charity* and learning bent,
   With open ears — and purses willing —
Where they could dry the orphan's tear,
And see the world, and speeches hear,
   All — "*for a matter of two shilling!*"

Let Envy drop her raven quill,
Let Slander's venom'd lip be still,
   And hush'd Detraction's croaking song!
That dar'd, devoid of taste and sense,
To call these sons of Eloquence,
   A stammering, spouting, schoolboy throng

'Tis false — for they in grave debate
Weigh'd mighty themes of church and state,
   With words of power, and looks of sages;
While, far-diffused, their gracious smile
Sooth'd Bony in his prison isle,
   And Turkish wives in Haram's cages!

Heaven bless 'em — for their generous pity
Toil'd hard to light our darkened city,
   With that firm zeal that never flinches;
And long, to prove the love they bore us,
With "*more last words*" they linger'd o'er us,
   And like a tom-cat, died by inches!!

                        CROAKER & Co.

ODE TO FORTUNE.

Fair lady with the bandag'd eye!
   I'll pardon all thy scurvy tricks,
So thou wilt *cut* me and deny
   Alike thy kisses and thy kicks:
I'm quite contented as I am —
   Have cash to keep my duns at bay,
Can choose between beef steaks and ham,
   And drink Madeira every day.

My station is the middle rank,
   My fortune — just a competence —
Ten thousand in the Franklin Bank,
   And twenty in the six per cents:
No amorous chains my heart enthrall,
   I neither borrow, lend, nor sell;
Fearless I roam the City Hall,
   And bite my thumb at Mr. Bell.[107]

The horse that twice a year I ride,
　　At Mother Dawson's[108] eats his fill;
My books at Goodrich's[109] abide,
　　My country seat is Wehawk hill;
My morning lounge is Eastburn's[110] shop,
　　At Poppleton's I take my lunch;
Niblo prepares my mutton chop,
　　And Jennings[111] makes my whiskey punch.

When merry, I the hours amuse
　　By squibbing Bucktails, Guards, and Balls;
And when I'm troubled with the blues,
　　Damn Clinton, and abuse Canals:
Then Fortune! since I ask no prize,
　　At least preserve me from thy frown;
The man who don't attempt to rise,
　　'Twere cruelty to tumble down.

　　　　　　　　　　CROAKER & CO.

THE LOVE OF NOTORIETY.

> "'Tis pleasant, through the loopholes of retreat,
> To peep at such a world."
>   Cowper.

There are laurels our temples throb warmly to claim,
   Unwet by the blood-dripping fingers of war;
And as dear to the heart are the *whispers* of fame,
   As the blasts of her bugle rang fiercely and far.
The death-dirge is sung o'er the warrior's tomb,
   Ere the world to his valor its homage will give:
But the feathers that form Notoriety's plume,
   Are plucked in the sunshine, and bright while we live.

There's a wonderful charm in that sort of renown,
Which consists in becoming "*the talk of the town;*"
'Tis a pleasure which none but "*your truly great*" feels,
To be followed about by a mob at one's heels;
And to hear, from the gazing and mouth-open throng,
The dear words, "*that's he,*" as one trudges along;
While Beauty, all anxious, stands up on tip-toes,
Leans on her beau's shoulders, and lisps "*there he goes.*"

For this, the young Dandy, half whalebone, half starch,
Parades Broadway, with the true Steuben march;
A new species of being — created, they say,
By nine London tailors, who ventured one day
To *cabbage* a spark of Promethean fire,
Which they placed in a German doll stiffen'd with wire,
And formed of the scare-crow a Dandy divine.
But *mum* about tailors — I have n't paid mine.

And for this, little *Brummagem* mounts with a smile,
His *own hackney* buggy — and dashes in style
   From some livery stable to Cato's[112] hotel.
And, though 'tis a desperate task to be striving
With these sons of John Bull in the *science* of driving,
   We have still a few others that do it as well.
There are, too, "*par example,*" 'tis joy to behold,
   With their Haytian grooms trotting graceful behind
      'em,
In their livery jackets of blue, green and gold,
   Their bright-varnish'd hats, and the laces that bind 'em,
The one's an Adonis — who since the sad day
   That he shot at himself,[113] has been counted no more;
The other's a name it were treason to say,
   A very great man — with two lamps[114] at his door.

CROAKER & CO.

When the Western District was surveyed, the power of naming the townships was entrusted to the Surveyor-General. Finding the Indian appellations too sonorous and poetical, and that his own ear was not altogether adapted for the musical combination of syllables, this gentleman hit upon a plan, which for laughable absurdity, has never been paralleled, except by the "Philosophy," "Philanthropy," and "Big Little Dry" system of Lewis & Clarke. It was no other, than selecting from Lempriere and the British Plutarch, the great names which those works commemorate. This plan he executed with the most ridiculous fidelity, and reared for himself an everlasting monument of pedantry and folly.

AN ODE
TO SIMEON DE WITT,[115] ESQUIRE,
SURVEYOR-GENERAL.

If, on the deathless page of Fame,
   The warrior's deeds are writ;
If that bright record bear the name
Of each, whose hallowed brow might claim
   The wreath of wisdom or of wit:
If ever they, whose cash and care
Have nurst the infant arts, be there,
   What place remains for thee?
Who, neither warrior, bard, nor sage,
Hast pour'd on this benighted age,
   The blended light of all the three.

God-father of the christen'd West!
   Thy wonder-working power
Has call'd from their eternal rest,
The poets and the chiefs who blest
   Old Europe in her happier hour:
Thou givest, to the buried great,
A citizen's certificate,
   And, aliens now no more,
The children of each classic town
Shall emulate their sire's renown
   In science, wisdom, or in war.

The bard who treads on *Homer's* earth
   Shall mount the epic throne,
And pour like breezes of the north,
Such spirit-stirring stanzas forth
   As Paulding would not blush to own!
And he, who casts around his eyes
Where *Hampden's* bright stone-fences rise,
   Shall swear with thrilling joint,
(As German[116] did,) "we yet are free,
And this accursed *tax* should be
   Resisted at the bayonet's point."

What man, where *Scipio's* praises skip
   From every rustling leaf,
But girds cold iron on his hip,
With "shoulder firelock!" arms his lip,
   And struts, a bold militia chief!

And who, that breathes where *Cato* lies,
But feels the Censor spirit rise
 At folly's idle pranks;
With voice that fills the Congress Halls,
"Domestic manufactures" bawls,[117]
 And damns the Dandies and the Banks.

Behold! where *Junius town* is set,
 A Brutus is the Judge;
'Tis true, he serves the Tarquin yet,
Still winds his limbs in folly's net,
 And seems a very patient drudge.
But let the Despot fall, and bright
As morning from the shades of night,
 Forth in his pride he'll stand,
The guard and glory of our soil!
A head for thought, a hand for toil,
 A tongue to warn, persuade, command.

Lo! Galen sends her *Doctors* round,
 Proficients in their trade;
Historians are in Livy found,
Ulysses, from her teeming ground,
 Pours *Politicians*, ready made;
Fresh *Orators* in *Tully* rise,
Nestor, our *Counsellors* supplies,
 Wise, vigilant, and close;
Gracchus, our *tavern-statesmen* rears,
And *Milton* finds us *pamphleteers*,
 As well as poets by the groce.

Surveyor of the western plains!
   The sapient work is thine—
Full-fledged, it sprung from out thy brains;
One added touch, alone, remains
   To consummate the grand design,
Select a town—and christen it
With thy unrivall'd name, De Witt!
   Soon shall the glorious bantling bless us
With a fair progeny of *Fools*,
To fill our colleges and schools
   With tutors, regents and professors.

CROAKER & CO.

TO E. SIMPSON, ESQ.,

MANAGER OF THE THEATRE.

Dear Neddy, since the day is near,
    Destined to close your late campaign,
'Tis well to note the coming year,
And learn how best you may appear
    Before the public eye again.
One thing at least, whate'er you do,
For God's sake give us something new.
For though your actors have not lost
    One candle-snuff of Thespian fire,
Yet beauties, that delight us most,
    The wearied eye, in time, will tire.
'Tis thus the sated gaze of taste
    Holland's [118] drop-curtain heedless passes,
And thus the school-boy loathes, at last,
    His sugar-candy and molasses.

Now if you will but take advice,
    Bank notes shall fall like summer rain,
And, next year, you and Mr. Price
    May *cut* your Claret for Champagne.
Just hand your present corps down stairs,
    Disband them all — and then create
Another army from the players
    That figure on the *stage of state*.
A better set there can not be
    For *clap-trap* and *stage-trickery*.
And they'll be well content to quit
    Their present post for higher pay;
For if they but good salaries get,
    It matters not what parts they play.
You'll have no quarrelling about
The *characters* you deal them out;
Their public acts too well have shown
They care but little for *their own*.

How nicely now would Spencer[119] fit
For "Overreach" and "Bajazet;"
Van Buren, tricky, sly, and thin,
Would make a noble "Harlequin;"
Clinton would play "King Dick" the surly,[120]
The learned "Pangloss," and grave "Lord Burleigh;"
Woodworth[121] (whose name the Muse shall hallow),
Is quite at home in "Justice Shallow;"
And slippery, smooth-faced Tallmadge[122] stands
A "Joseph Surface" to your hands.

THE CROAKERS.

Lo! where the *acting council*[123] sits,
A grand triumvirate of wits,
Cut out express by Nature's chisel,
For " Noodle, Doodle and Lord Grizzle ;"
The *Members* who contriv'd to fill
The state purse from the steamboat[124] till,
Dressed out in turbans and white sleeves,
Would figure in the " Forty Thieves."
We'll linger with delightful grin,
To see old Root in " Nipperkin ;"
And gaze, with reverential wonder,
On Skinner's[125] sapient face in "Ponder ;"
While Peter R——,[126] the jovial soul,
Will toss off "Jobson's" brimming bowl,
  Fit for a Senator to swim in ;
And *bravos*, rung from half the town,
Shall tell the fame of Walter Bowne[127]
  In " Cacafogo," and old women.

Our *City Aldermen*, you know,
Are conjurors, *ex officio* ;
And with the Mayor in his silk breeches,
Would do for " Hecate and the witches."
Christian and Warner,[128] long the scourges
  Of Bucks and other "*ragrom men*,"
Would find in " Dogberry and Verges"
  Their very selves restored again.

Buckmaster,[129] fat, and full of glee,
    Might rival Cooke in "Jack Falstaff;"
"Pistol" and "Bobadil" would be
    Revived once more in Captain Haff.
To classic Meigs, who soon — thank Heaven!
    In congress will illume the age;
The highest wages should be given
    To trim the lamps and *light* the stage.
Van Wyck[130] will play the "Giant Wife,"
And "Death in Blue Beard" — to the life;
And surly German[131] do, at least,
For "Bear" in "Beauty and the Beast."

Maxwell[132] and Gardenier, you'll fix,
    With strong indentures, by all means;
They're used to *shifting* politics,
    And soon would learn to *shift* the scenes.
Bacon might bustle on in "Meddler,"
Gilbert[133] play new tricks in "Diddler;"
    Good, honest Peter H. Wendover,[134]
In "Vortex" read his own speech over;
While Pell would strike the critics dumb,
A perfect miniature "Tom Thumb;"
And Mitchill, as in all the past,
    Talk science, and cut corns in "Last."[135]

                      CROAKER & Co.

For the New York Evening Post.

TO * * * *

Air—*Shannon Side.*

The world is bright before thee,
    Its summer flowers are thine,
Its calm blue sky is o'er thee,
    Thy bosom, Pleasure's shrine;
And thine the sunbeam given
    To Nature's morning hour,
Pure, warm, as when from heaven
    It burst on Eden's bower.

There is a song of sorrow,
    The death-dirge of the gay,
That tells, ere dawn of morrow,
    These charms may melt away;
That sun's bright beam be shaded,
    That sky be blue no more,
The summer flowers be faded,
    And youth's warm promise o'er.

Believe it not — though lonely
   Thy evening home may be,
Though Beauty's bark can only
   Float on a summer sea;
Though time thy bloom is stealing,
   There's still beyond his art,
The wild-flower wreath of feeling,
   The sunbeam of the heart.

                      CROAKER & Co.

THE COUNCIL OF APPOINTMENT.[137]

"*Off with his head!— so much for Buckingham.*"
                                        Shakspeare.

There's magic in the robe of power,
  Ennobling every thing beneath it;
Its spell is like the Upas' bower,
  Whose air will *puff up* all who breathe it.
Alike it charms the horse-hair tress
  That turkey's three-tailed Bashaws wear,
And hallow Clinton's levee dress,
  Cut by the classic shears of Baehr.[138]

Before its witchery — of late,
  Our proudest politicians trembled;
When the five Heads that rule the state
  Around the Council board assembled.
There, arbiter of fates and fortunes,
  Of brains it well supplied the loss,
Gave Bates[139] and Rosencrantz[140] importance,
  And made a gentleman of Ross![141]

'Tis vain to win a great man's name,
    Without some *proof* of having been one,
And *Killings* a sure path to fame,
    Vide Jack Ketch and Mr. Clinton!
Our Council well this path have trod,
    Honor's immortal wreath securing,
They've dipped their hatchets in the blood,
    The patriot blood of Mat. Van Buren.[16]

He bears, as every hero ought,
    The mandate of the powers that rule
(*He's* higher game in view, 'tis thought,
    All in good time; the man's no fool).
With him, some dozens prostrate fall,
    No friend to mourn, nor foe to flout them,
They die unsung, unwept by all,
    For no one cares a *sous* about them!

Wortman and Scott may grace the bar again,
    For them, a blest exchange we make;
We've dignity in Ned McGarraghan,
    We've *every thing* in Jerry Drake.
And lo! the wreath of wither'd leaves
    That lately twined Van Buren's brow,
Oakley's pure, spotless hand receives;
    He's earned it — 'tis no matter how!

THE CROAKERS.

Let office holders cease to weep,
    And put once more their gala dress on,
The Council's closed, and they may sleep
    In quiet, 'till the winter session.
Since all, or in, or out of place,
    Wear Knavery's cloak or Folly's feather,
'Tis ours, their *ups* and *downs* to trace,
    And laugh at *ins* and *outs* together.

CROAKER & CO.

Friday, 6 o'clock.

Mr. Coleman: The extravagant price of Leghorn hats in London, as mentioned in your paper this evening, suggests the annexed lines.

You will observe, that part of the first stanza is an almost literal quotation from Milton.

Yours,

Croaker.

CURTAIN CONVERSATIONS.[113]

"I will pay no debts of her contracting after this date."
Daily Newspapers.

"Beside the nuptial curtain bright,"
  The bard of Eden sings,
"Young Love his constant lamp will light,
  And wave his purple wings."
But rain-drops, from the clouds of care,
  May bid that lamp be dim,
And the boy Love will pout and swear
  'Tis then no place for him.

So mus'd the lovely Mrs. Dash
  (We blush to mention names),
When for her surly husband's cash
  She urg'd, in vain, her claims.
"I want a little money, dear,
  "As Vandervoort and Flandin,"[114]
"Their bill (which now has run a year)
  "To-morrow mean to hand in."

"Zounds!"[115] cried the husband, half asleep,
  "You'll drive me to despair."
The lady was too proud to weep,
  And too polite to swear:
She bit her lip for very spite;
  He felt a storm was brewing,
And dream'd of nothing else all night
  But brokers, banks and ruin!

He thought her pretty once — but dreams
  Have sure a wond'rous power;
For, to his eye, the lady seems
  Quite altered since that hour.
And Love, who, on their bridal eve,
  Had promised long to stay,
Forgot his promise, took *French leave*,
  And bore his lamp away.

CROAKER & Co.

AN ADDRESS[116]

FOR THE OPENING OF THE NEW THEATRE, TO BE SPOKEN BY MR. OLLIFF.[117]

Ladies and Gentlemen:

   Enlighten'd as you are, you all must know
Our play house was burnt down, some time ago,
Without insurance [118] — 'Twas a famous blaze,
Fine fun for firemen, but dull sport for plays;
The proudest of our whole dramatic *corps*
Such *warm reception* never met before.
It was a woful night for us and ours,
Worse than dry weather to the fields and flowers,
The evening found us gay as summer's lark,
   Happy as sturgeons in the Tappan sea;
The morning — like the dove from Noah's ark,
   As homeless, houseless, innocent as she.
But — thanks to those who ever have been known
To love the public interest — when their own;
Thanks to the men of talent and of trade,
Who joy in doing well — when they're well paid,
Again our fireworn mansion is rebuilt,
Inside and outside, neatly carv'd and gilt,
With best of paint and canvas, lath and plaster,
The Lord bless Beekman and John Jacob Astor.[119]

As an old coat, from Jennings' [150] patent screw,
Comes out clean-scour'd and brighter than the new,
As an old head in Saunders' [151] patent wig,
Looks wiser than when young, and twice as big,
As Mat. Van Buren, in the Senate Hall,
Repairs the loss we met in Spencer's fall,
As the new constitution will (we're told)
Be worth at least a dozen of the old —
So is our new house better than its brother,
Its roof is painted yellower than the other,
It is insur'd at three per cent. 'gainst fire,
And cost three times as much, and is six inches higher.

'Tis not alone the house — The prompter's clothes
Are all quite new — so are the fiddlers' bows;
The supernumeraries are newly shav'd,
New drill'd, and all extremely well behav'd,
(They'll each one be allow'd (I stop to mention)
The right of suffrage by the new convention);
We've some new thunder, several new plays,
And a new splendid carpet of green baize.
So that there's nought remains to bid us reach
The topmost bough of favor — but a speech —
A speech — the prelude to each public meeting,
Whether for morals, charity or eating;
A speech — the modern mode of winning hearts,
And power, and fame, in politics and arts.

What made the good Monroe our President?
'Twas that through all this blessed land he went
With his immortal cock'd hat and short breeches,
Dining wherever ask'd — and making speeches.
What, when Missouri stood on her last legs,
Revived her hopes? — the speech of Henry Meigs.[152]
What proves our country learned, wise and happy?
Mitchill's Address to the Phi Beta Kappa.
What has convinced the world that we have men
First with the sword, the chisel, brush and pen,
Shaming all English Authors, men or madams?
The Fourth of July speech of Mr. Adams.
Yes — If our managers grow great and rich,
And players prosper — let them thank my speech,[153]
And let the name of Olliff proudly go
With Meigs and Adams, Mitchill and Monroe.

TO WALTER BOWNE, ESQ.,[154]

SENATOR OF THE STATE OF NEW YORK, MEMBER OF THE COUNCIL OF APPOINTMENT,[155] &C. &C. &C., AT ALBANY IN THE SPRING OF 1821.

" I can not but remember that such things were,
And were most precious to me."
Shakspeare.

We do not blame you, Walter Bowne,
   For a variety of reasons,
You're now the talk of half the town,
A man of talent and renown,
   And will be, for perhaps two seasons.
That face of yours has magic in it,
Its smile transports us in a minute,
   To wealth and pleasure's sunny bowers:
And there is terror in its frown,
Which, like a mower's scythe, cuts down
   Our city's loveliest flowers.

We, therefore, do not blame you, sir,
   Whate'er our cause of grief may be,
And cause enough we have to stir
   The very stones to mutiny.

You've driven from the cash and cares
Of office, heedless of our prayers,
Men who have been, for many a year,
To us, and to our purses dear,
    And will be to our heirs for ever.
Our tears, aided by snow and rain,
Have swelled the brook in Maiden lane
    Into a mountain river;
And when you visit us again,
Leaning at Tammany on your cane,
Like warrior on his battle-blade,
You'll mourn the havoc you have made.

There is a silence and a sadness
    Within the marble mansion now;
Some have wild eyes that look like madness,
    Some talk of kicking up a row.
Judge Miller will not yet believe
That you have ventured to bereave
    The city and its hall of him;
He has in his own fine way stated,
"The fact must be substantiated,"
    Before he'll move a single limb.
He thinks it cursed hard to yield
The laurel won in every field,
    Through sixteen years of party war,
And to be seen at noon no more
Enjoying, at his office door,
    The luxury of a tenth segar

Judge Warner says that, now he's gone,
  We've lost the true Dogberry breed;
And Christian swears that you have done
  A most *un*-Christian deed.

How could you have the heart to strike
From place the peerless Pierre Van Wyck?
And the two colonels, Haines[136] and Pell,
Squire Fessenden and Sheriff Bell?[137]
Morrell, a justice, and a wise one,
And Ned M'Laughlin, the exciseman?
The two health officers, believers
In Clinton and contagious fevers?
The keeper of the city's treasures,
The sealer of her weights and measures?
  The harbor master, her best bower
  Cable in party's stormy hour?
Ten auctioneers, three bank directors,
And Mott and Duffy, the inspectors
  Of whiskey and of flour?

It was but yesterday they stood
All (*ex officio*) great and good —
But by the tomahawk struck down
Of party, and of Walter Bowne,
Where are they now? — with shapes of air,
The caravans of things that were,
Journeying to their nameless home
Like Mecca's pilgrims from her tomb —

With the lost Pleiad — with the wars
Of Agamemnon's ancestors —
With their own years of joy and grief,
Spring's bud and autumn's faded leaf,
With birds that round their cradles flew,
With winds that in their boyhoods blew,
With last night's dream and last night's dew.

Yes, they are gone, alas, each one of them,
Departed, every mother's son of them.
Yet, often, at the close of day,
When thoughts are winged and wandering, they
Come with the memory of the past,
  Like sunset clouds along the wind,
Reflecting, as they're flitting fast,
In their wild hues of shade and light,
All that was beautiful and bright,
  In golden moments left behind.

THE RECORDER.[158]

A POETICAL EPISTLE.

BY THOMAS CASTALY.

---

*"On they move
In perfect phalanx to the Dorian mood
Of flutes and soft* RECORDERS.*"*
                                Milton.

"Live in Settles numbers one day more!"
                                Pope.

My dear Dick Riker,[159] you and I
    Have floated down life's stream together,
And kept unharmed our friendship's tie,
Through every change of fortune's sky,
    Her pleasant and her rainy weather.
Full sixty times since first we met,
Our birth-day suns have risen and set,
And time has worn the baldness now
Of Julius Cæsar on your brow;

Your brow — like his, a field of thought,
With broad deep furrows, spirit-wrought,
Whose laurel harvests long have shone
As green and glorious as his own;
And proudly would the CÆSAR claim
Companionship with RIKER'S name,
His peer in forehead and in fame.
Both eloquent and learned and brave,
  Born to command and skilled to rule,
One made the citizen a slave,
  The other makes him more — a fool.
The CÆSAR an imperial crown,
  His slaves' mad gift, refused to wear;
The RIKER put his fool's cap on,
  And found it fitted to a hair.
The CÆSAR, though by birth and breeding,
Travel, the ladies, and light reading,
A gentleman in mien and mind,
  And fond of Romans and their mothers,
Was heartless as the Arab's wind,
And slew some millions of mankind,
  Including enemies and others.
The RIKER, like Bob Acres, stood
Edge-ways upon a field of blood,
  The where and wherefore Swartwout[100] knows,
Pulled trigger, as a brave man should,
  And shot, God bless them — his own toes.

The CÆSAR passed the Rubicon
  With helm and shield and breast plate on,
Dashing his war-horse through the waters;
  The RIKER would have built a barge
  Or steam boat, at the city's charge,
And passed it with his wife and daughters.
But let that pass. As I have said,
There's nought, save laurels, on your head,
And time has changed my clustering hair,
And showered the snow flakes thickly there,
And though our lives have ever been,
As different as their different scene;
Mine more renowned for rhymes than riches,
Your's less for scholarship than speeches;
Mine passed in low-roofed leafy bower,
Your's in high halls of pomp and power,
Yet are we, be the moral told,
Alike in one thing — growing old;
Ripened like summer's cradled sheaf,
Faded like Autumn's falling leaf —
And nearing, sail and signal spread,
The quiet anchorage of the dead;
For such is human life, wherever
  The voyage of its bark may be,
On home's green-banked and gentle river,
  Or the world's shoreless, sleepless sea.

Yes, you have floated down the tide
Of time, a SWAN in grace and pride

And majesty and beauty, till
The law, the Ariel of your will,
  Power's best beloved, the law of libel
(A bright link in the feudal chain)
Expounded, settled, and made plain,
  By your own charge, the Jurors' Bible,
Has clipped the venomed tongue of Slander,
That dared to call you "Party's GANDER,
"The leader of the geese who make
  "Our city's parks and ponds their home,
"And keep her liberties awake
  "By cackling, as their sires saved Rome.
"GANDER of Party's pond, wherein
"Lizard, and toad, and terrapin,
"Your ale-house patriots, are seen,
  "In Faction's feverish sunshine basking."
And now, to rend this veil of lies,
Word-woven by your enemies,
And keep your sainted memory free,
From tarnish with posterity,
  I take the liberty of asking
Permission, sir, to write your life,
With all its scenes of calm and strife,
  And all its turnings and its windings,
A poem in a quarto volume,
Verse like the subject, blank and solemn,
  With elegant appropriate bindings,
Of rat and mole skin the one half,
The other a part fox, part calf.

Your portrait graven line for line,
From that immortal bust in plaster,
The master piece of Art's great Master,
   Mr. Praxiteles Browere,
Whose trowel is a thing divine,
Shall smile and bow, and promise there,
And twenty-nine fine forms and faces,
   The Corporation and the Mayor,
Linked hand in hand, like Loves and Graces,
   Shall hover o'er it grouped in air
With wild pictorial dance and song;
   The song, of happy bees in bowers,
   The dance of Guido's graceful hours,
   All scattering Flushing's garden flowers
Round the dear head they've loved so long.

I know that you are modest, know
   That when you hear your merit's praise,
Your cheek's quick blushes come and go,
Lily and rose-leaf, sun and snow,
   Like maidens' on their bridal days.
I know that you would fain decline
To aid me and the sacred Nine,
In giving to the asking Earth,
The story of your wit and worth;
For if there be a fault to cloud
   The brightness of your clear good sense,
It is, and be the fact allowed,
   Your only failing — DIFFIDENCE!

An amiable weakness — given
    To justify the sad reflection,
That in this vale of tears not even
    A Riker is complete perfection.
A most romantic detestation
Of power and place, of pay and ration;
A strange unwillingness to carry
    The weight of honor on your shoulders,
For which you have been named, the very
    Sensitive-plant of office holders.
A shrinking bashfulness, whose grace
Gives beauty to your manly face.
Thus shades the green and growing vine,
The rough bark of the mountain pine,
Thus round her Freedom's waking steel
    Harmodius wreathed his country's myrtle;
And thus the golden lemon's peel
    Gives fragrance to a bowl of turtle.

True "many a flower," the poet sings,
    "Is born to blush unseen,"
But you, although you blush, are not
    The flower the poets mean.
In vain you wooed a lowlier lot,
    In vain you clipt your eagle-wings;
Talents like yours are not forgot
    And buried with Earth's common things.
No! my dear Riker, I would give
My laurels, living and to live,

Or as much cash as you could raise on
Their value, by hypothecation,
To be, for one enchanted hour,
In beauty, majesty, and power,
What you for forty years have been,
The Oberon of life's fairy scene!

An anxious city sought and found you
   In a blest day of joy and pride,
Sceptered your jewelled hand, and crowned you
   Her chief, her guardian, and her guide.
Honors which weaker minds had wrought
   In vain for years, and knelt and prayed for,
Are all your own, unpriced, unbought,
   Or (which is the same thing) unpaid for.
Painfully great! against your will
   Her hundred offices to hold,
Each chair with dignity to fill,
   And your own pockets, with her gold.
A sort of double duty, making
Your task a serious undertaking.

With what delight, the eyes of all
Gaze on you, seated in your HALL,[161]
   Like Sancho in his island, reigning,
Lord leader of its motley hosts
Of lawyers and their bills of costs,
   And all things thereto appertaining,

Such as crimes, constables and juries,
Male pilferers and female furies,
The police and the *Pollissons*,
Illegal right and legal wrong.
Bribes, perjuries, law-craft and cunning,
Judicial drollery and punning;
And all the *et ceteras* that grace
That genteel, gentlemanly place!
Or in the Council Chamber standing,
   With eloquence of eye and brow,
Your voice the music of commanding,
   And fascination in your bow,
Arranging for the civic shows
   Your "men in buckram," as per list,
Your John Does and your Richard Roes,
   Those Dummys of your games of whist.
The Council Chamber — where authority
Consists in two words — a majority.
For whose contractors' jobs we pay
   Our last dear sixpences for taxes,
As freely as in Sylla's day,
   Rome bled beneath his lictors' axes.
Where — on each magisterial nose
   In colors of the rainbow linger,
Like sunset hues on Alpine snows,
   The printmarks of your thumb and finger.
Where he, the wisest of wild fowl,
Bird of Jove's blue-eyed maid — the owl,

That feathered alderman, is heard
Nightly, by poet's ear alone,
To others' eyes and ears unknown,
   Cheering your every look and word.
And making, room and gallery through,
   The loud, applauding echoes peal,
Of his "*où peut on être mieux
Qu'au sein de sa famille.*"[162]
Oh! for a Herald's skill to rank
   Your titles in their due degrees!
At Sing Sing — at the Tradesmen's Bank,
   In courts, committees, caucuses:
At Albany, where those who know
   The last year's secrets of the Great,
Call you the golden handle to
   The earthen PITCHER of the State.
(Poor Pitcher![163] that Van Buren ceases
   To want its service gives me pain,
'Twill break into as many pieces
   As Kitty's of Coleraine.)
At Bellevue,[164] on her banquet night,
   Where Burgundy and business meet,
On others, at the heart's delight,
   The Pewter Mug[165] in Frankfort street,
From Harlem bridge to Whitehall dock,
   From Bloomingdale to Blackwell's isles,
Forming, including road and rock,
   A city of some twelve square miles,

O'er street and alley, square and block,
    Towers, temples, telegraphs and tiles,
O'er wharves whose stone and timbers mock
The ocean's and its navies' shock,
O'er all the fleets that float before her,
O'er all their banners waving o'er her,
Her sky and waters, earth and air —
You are Lord, for who is her LORD MAYOR?
Where is he? Echo answers, where?
And voices, like the sound of seas
Breathe in sad chorus, on the breeze,
The Highland mourner's melody —
Oh HONE[166] a rie! O HONE a rie!
The hymn o'er happy days departed,
    The hope that such again may be,
When power was large and liberal-hearted,
    And wealth was hospitality.

One more request, and I am lost
    If you its earnest prayer deny,
It is that you preserve the most
    Inviolable secrecy
As to my plan. Our fourteen wards
Contain some thirty-seven bards,
Who, if my glorious theme were known,
Would make it, thought and word, their own,
My hopes and happiness destroy,
And trample with a rival's joy

Upon the grave of my renown.
My younger brothers in the art,
Whose study is the human heart —
Minstrels, before whose spells have bowed
The learned, the lovely, and the proud —
　Ere their life's morning hours are gone
Free minds be theirs, the Muse's boon,
And may their suns blaze bright at noon,
　And set without a cloud.

HILLHOUSE, whose music like his themes
Lifts earth to Heaven — whose poet-dreams
Are pure and holy as the hymn
Echoed from harps of seraphim,
By bards that drank at Zion's fountains
　When glory, peace, and hope were hers,
And beautiful upon her mountains
　The feet of angel messengers.
Bryant, whose songs are thoughts that bless
　The heart, its teachers, and its joy,
As mothers blend with their caress
Lessons of truth and gentleness
　And virtue for the listening boy.
Spring's lovelier flowers for many a day
Have blossomed on his wandering way —
Being of beauty and decay,
　They slumber in their autumn tomb;
But those who graced his own GREEN RIVER,
　And wreathed the lattice of his home,

Charmed by his song from mortal doom,
   Bloom on, and will bloom on forever.
And HALLECK — who has made thy roof,
St Tammany! oblivion-proof —
Thy beer illustrious, and thee
A belted knight of chivalry;
And changed thy dome of painted bricks,
And porter casks, and politics,
   Into a green Arcadian vale,
With Stephen Allen[167] for its lark,
Ben Bailey's voice its watch dog's bark
   And John Targee,[168] its nightingale.

These, and the other thirty-four,
Will live a thousand years or more —
If the world lasts so long. For me,
I rhyme not for posterity,
Though pleasant to my heirs might be
   The incense of its praise,
When I, their ancestor, have gone
And paid the debt, the only one
   A poet ever pays.
But many are my years, and few
Are left me ere night's holy dew,
And sorrow's holier tears, will keep
The grass green where in death I sleep.
And when that grass is green above me,
And those who bless me now and love me
   Are sleeping by my side,

Will it avail me aught that men
Tell to the world with lip and pen
   That once I lived and died?
No — if a garland for my brow
Is growing, let me have it now,
   While I'm alive to wear it;
And if, in whispering my name,
There's music in the voice of fame,
   Like Garcia's, let me hear it!

The Christmas holidays are nigh,
Therefore, 'till New-Year's Eve, good bye,
   Then *revenons a nos moutons*,
Yourself and Aldermen'— meanwhile,
Look o'er this letter with a smile;
And keep the secret of its song
As faithfully, but not as long,
As you have guarded from the eyes
Of editorial Paul Prys,
   And other meddling, murmuring claimants,
Those Eleusinian mysteries.
   The City's cash receipts and payments.

                 Yours ever,
                       T. C.

For the Evening Post.[169]

EPISTLE TO ROBERT HOGBIN, ESQ.

ONE OF THE COMMITTEE OF WORKING MEN, &C., AT THE WESTCHESTER HOTEL, BOWERY.

Mr. Hogbin, I work as a weaver of rhyme,
    And therefore presume, with a working man's grace,
To address you, as one I have liked for some time,
    Though I know not (no doubt its a fine one) your face.

There is much in a name, and I'll lay you a wager
    (Two small jugs from Reynolds[170]), that Nature designed,
When she found you, that you should become the drum major,
    In that sweet piece of music the Grand March of Mind.

A Hogbin! a Hogbin! how cheering the shout
    Of all that keep step to that beautiful air
Which leads, like the Treadmill, about and about,
    And leaves us exactly, at last, where we were.

Yes, there's much in a name, and a HOGBIN so fit is
    For that great moral purpose whose impulse divine,
Bids men leave their own workshops to work in committees,
    And their own wedded wives to protect yours and mine.

That we working men prophets are sadly mistaken,
    If yours is not, HOGBIN, a durable fame,
Immortal as England's philosopher Bacon,
    Whom your ancestors housed, if we judge by his name.

When the moment arrives that we've won the good fight,
    And broken the chains of laws, churches and marriages,
When no infants are born under six feet in height,
    And our chimney sweeps mount up a flue in their carriages.

That glorious time, when our daughters and sons
    Enjoy a *Blue Monday* each day of the week,
And a clean shirt is classed with the mastodon's bones,
    Or a mummy from Thebes, an undoubted antique.

Then, then, my dear HOGBIN, your statue in straw,
    By some modern Pygmalion delightfully wrought,
Shall be placed in the Park, and our youths' only law
    Shall be to be HOGBINS in feeling and thought!

Yours,
A WORKING MAN.

THE DINNER PARTY.

Johnny R——[171] gave a dinner last night,
    The best I have tasted this season,
The wine and the wit sparkled bright,
    'Twas a frolic of soul and of reason.
For the guests, there were Cooper[172] and Kean,[173]
    Bishop Hobart,[174] and Alderman Brasher,
And Buchanan,[175] that foe to the queen,
    And Sherred, the painter and glazier.

The beef had been warm, it is true,
    But when we sat down, it was colder;
The wine when we entered was new,
    When we drank it, 'twas six hours older.
Mr. Kean, by the way he's no dunce,
    His plate was so often repeating,
I thought he'd a genius at once,
    Not only for acting, but eating.

Mr. Cooper, a sensible man,
    Talked much of his scheme of rebuilding
The theatre on a new plan,
    With fantastical carving and gilding.
Says he, "I've a thought of my own;
    Of the people, so stupid the taste is,
I could fill the new play house in June
    If I only could furnish new faces."

In addition to those I have named,
    Harry Cruger[176] was there in his glory,
That *ci-devant jeune homme* so famed
    In Paris — but that's an old story.
And General Lewis,[177] by Jove!
    With two vests, and a new fashioned eye-glass,
He looked like the young god of love
    At distance, beheld through a spy-glass;

I have read my first stanza again
    And find that for once I have erred,
For Robert and Mat were the men,
    Instead of Buchanan and Sherred.
Two Frenchmen, the best I have met,
    At home, in bad English and flummery,
Were there — just to make up the set,
    Together with Master Montgomery.[178]

Jack Nicholson[179] wanted to come
    With his pea-jacket on, but the ladies
Compelled him to leave it at home;
    So he wore, as becoming his trade is,
Two epaulets — one on each arm,
    And a sword, once of laurels the winner,
Ever ready in case of alarm,
    At carving a foe or a dinner.

Bishop Hobart said grace with an air,
    'Twould have done your heart good to have seen him,
And Lewis, so sweetly did swear,
    You'd have thought that the devil was in him.
And Alderman Brasher[180] began
    A song, but he could not go through it:
When Johnny R—— asks me again
    To a fête, by the Lord, I'll go to it.

II.

THE TEA PARTY.

The tea-urn is singing, the tea cups are gay,
    The fire sparkles bright in the room of D. K.[18]
For the first time these six months, a broom has been
    there,
    And the housemaid has brushed every table and chair;
Drugs, minerals, books, are all hidden from view,
    And the five shabby pictures are varnished anew;
There's a feast going on, there's the devil to pay
    In the furnished apartments of Doctor D. K.

What magic has raised all this bustle and noise,
    Disturbing the bachelor's still quiet joys;
A pair of young witches have doomed them to death,
    They are distant relations to those in Macbeth.
Not as ugly 'tis true, but as mischievious quite,
    And like them in teasing and taking delight;
This morning they sent him a billet to say,
    To night we take tea with you, Doctor D. K.

There is Mrs. I. D. in her high glee and glory,
　　And E. McC. with her song and her story;
There's a smile on each lip, and a leer on each brow,
　　And they both are determined to kick up a row;
They're mistaken for once, as they'll presently see,
　　For D. K.'s drinking whiskey with Langstaff and me;
They'll find the cage there, but the bird is away,
　　Catch a weazel asleep, and catch Doctor D. K.

　　　　　　　　　　　　　F. G. H. 1820.

THE MODERN HYDRA.

There is a beast sublime and savage,
    The Hydra by denomination;
Well doth he know his foes to ravage,
    And barks and bites to admiration.
Fox — wolf — cat — dog — of each, at least, he
    Has a full share, and never scants 'em;
But what is strangest in this beast, he
    Can make new heads whene'er he wants 'em.

For when our Tammany Alcides
    Had tomahawk'd his head political,
Straight from the bleeding trunk, out slid his
    Well fill'd noddle scientifical.
Another comes — another! see —
    They rise in infinite variety;
One cries aloud "Free school trustee!"
    The next exclaims, "Humane society!"

Behold the fourth — be-whiskered — big —
  A warlike cock'd hat frowns upon it;
The fifth uprears a doctor's wig!
  The sixth displays the judgment bonnet.
Herculean Noah! your strength you waste,
Reserve your furious cuts and slashes,
Till Satan stands beside the beast
  With red-hot steel to sear the gashes.

THE MEETING OF THE GROCERS.

The knights of the firkin are gathered around,
    The rag-idol's rights to assert;
Each gatherer pricks up his ears at the sound,
Town rags are advancing a penny a pound,
    While country rags sink in the dirt.

Aghast stand the brokers — the carrying trade
    Is lost if the butter-boys win;
The farmers are quaking — the west is dismayed,
Omnipotent Fundable trembles, afraid,
    And Wall street is all in a din.

'T wasn't so when the banks, in a body, prepared
    To cut their own corporate throats;
And biting their thumbs at the farmers, declared
To the thunderstruck dealers in butter and lard,
    They would handle no more of their notes.

Oh! Fundable, Fundable! look to thine own,
   Now, now, let thy management shine;
I fear the young Franklin will worry thee down,
And, if all the bad paper be kicked out of town,
   Dear Fundable! where will be thine?

THE KING OF THE DOCTORS.[182]

How stately your palace uplifts its proud head,
    Where Broadway and Barclay street meet;
Abhorring its old fashioned tunic of red,
It shines in the lustre of chromate of lead,
    And its doors open — into the street!

No longer it rings to the merry sleigh bells,[183]
    The steed's gallant neighings are o'er;
Instead of the pitchfork, we meet with scalpels,
And the throne of his medical majesty dwells
    Where the horse-trough resided before.

Oh! David! how dreadful and dire was the note,
    When Rebellion beleaguered the place;
When the bull-dog of discord unbolted his throat,
And the hot Digitales[184] unbuttoned his coat
    And doubled his fist in your face.

Then syncope seized thee — all wild with affright
  The Lord Chamberlain cried "God defend ye!"
Mac[185] swung his shillela in hopes of a fight,
While the brave Surgeon-General exclaimed in delight,
  "*Pugnatum est arte medendi.*"

But your wars are all ended, you're now at your ease,
  The Regents are bound for your debts;
You may fleece your poor students as much as you please,
Tax boldly, matriculate, double your fees,
  You can pay off all scores in brevets.

So a health to your highness, and long may you reign,
  Over subjects obedient and true;
If the snaffle wont hold them, apply the curb rein,
And if ever they prance, or go backward again,
  May you horsewhip them all black and blue.

MR. CLINTON'S SPEECH.

JANUARY, 1825.

———

To Tallmadge [ist] of the upper house,
   And Crolius [ist] of the lower,
After, "*non nobis Domine*,"
   Thus saith the Governor.

It seems by general admission,
   That, as a nation, we are thriving;
Settled in excellent condition,
   Bargaining, building, and bee-hiving.
That each one fearlessly reclines
Beneath his " fig tree and his vines,"
   (The dream of philosophic man),
And all is quiet as on Sunday
From Orleans to the Bay of Fundy,
   From Beersheba to Dan.

I've climbed my country's loftiest tree,
  And reached its highest bough — save one,
Why not the highest? — blame not me,
  "What men dare" do, I've done.
And though thy city, Washington,
  Still mocks my eagle wing and eye,
Yet is there joy upon a throne
  Even here at Albany.
For though but second in command,
  Far floats my banner in the breeze,
A Captain-General's on the land,
  An Admiral's on the seas.[188]
And, if Ambition can ask more,
My very title — Governor,
  A princely pride creates,
Because it gives me kindred claims
To greatness with those glorious names,
  A Sancho, and a Yates.

As party spirit has departed
  This life to breathe and blast no more,
The patriot and the honest hearted
  Shall form my diplomatic *corps*.
The wise, the talented, the good,
  Selected from my band of yore,
My own devoted band, who've stood
Beside me, stemming faction's flood,
  Like rocks on Ocean's shore.

Men, who, if now the field were lost,
    Again would buckle sword and mail on,
Followed by them, themselves a host,
Haines, Hurtell, Herring, Pell and Post,[129]
Judge Miller, Mumford, and Van Wyck,
'Tis said I look extremely like
    A Highland chieftain with his tail on.

A clear and comprehensive view
    Of every thing in art or nature,
In this my opening speech is due
    To an enlightened legislature.
I therefore have arranged with care,
    In orderly classification,
The following subjects, which should share
    Your most mature deliberation.

Physicians, senators, and makers
    Of patent medicines and machines,
The train-bands and the Shaking Quakers,
    Forts, colleges and quarantines,
Debts, cadets, coal mines and canals,
    Salt — the comptroller's next report,
Reform within our prison walls,
    The customs and the supreme court,
Delinquents, juvenile and gray,
    Schools, steam boats, justices of peace,
Republics of the present day,
    And those of Italy and Greece;

Militia officers, and they
    Who serve in the police —
Mad men and laws — a great variety,
The horticultural society,
The rate of interest and of tolls,
The number of tax-worthy souls,
    Roads — and a mail three times a week
From where the gentle Erie rolls
    To Conewango creek.

These are a few affairs of state
    On which I ask your reasoning powers,
High themes for study and debate
    For closet and for caucus hours.

This is my longest speech, but those
    Who feel, that, like a cable's strength,
    Its power increases with its length,
Will weep to hear its close.
Weep not — my next shall be as long,
And that, like this, — embalmed in song,
Will be, when two brief years are told,
    Mine own no longer, but the Nation's,
With all my speeches, new and old,
And what is more — the place I hold,
    Together with its pay and rations.

THE NIGHTMARE.

---

*"Sure he was sent from heaven express to be the pillar of the state.
So terrible his name, "Clintonian" nurses frighten children with it."*

Tom Thumb.

Dreaming last night — of Pierre Van Wyck,
   I felt the *nightmare* creeping o'er me;
In vain I strove to speak or strike,
   The horrid form was still before me:
Till, panting — struggling to be free,
   I raised my weak, but desperate head,
And faintly muttered "John Targee!"
   When — with a howl — the goblin fled.

I waked, and cried in glad surprise,
   The man is found, ordained by fate
To break our bonds, and exorcise
   The nightmare of the sleeping state.
He'll chase the demons, great and small,
   They'll sink his withering gaze before;
Then rouse! ye sachems at the Hall,
And nominate him Governor.

Up with the name on Freedom's cause,
    Inscribe it, Bucktails, on your banner;
Fame's pewter trump shall sound applause,
    And blasts from party's furnace fan her.
Pledge high his health in mugs of beer,
    And roaring like the boisterous sea,
Thunder in Clinton's frighted ear,
    The conquering name of John Targee!

TO THE
DIRECTORS OF THE ACADEMY OF ARTS.

WRITTEN ON VISITING THE FIRST EXHIBITION IN 1816.

Illustrious autocrats of taste!
Inspectors of the wonders traced
   By pencil, brush or chisel;
Accept a nameless poet's lay
Who longs to twine a twig of bay
   Around his penny whistle.

Ye learned and enlightened few
Who keep the portal of *virtu*,
   I pray you now unlock it;
And grant a peep for all my pains,
Within your oil-bedaubed domains,
Where now the poor in brains
   Succeed the poor in pocket.

Immortal be the rich repast,
At which the sage decree was past,
   Of pauper health so tender;
Which sent the beggars to Bellevue,
And left the classic fane to you
   And Scudder's witch of Endor.

Obliging all, you fear no harm
From disappointment's angry arm,
   No cudgels, sneers or libels;
Alike you smile on worst and best,
From great Rubens and quaker West,
   To wooden cuts for Bibles.

Lo! next the Gallic thunderbolt,
Some nameless, shapeless, ugly dolt,
   His plastic phiz advances;
And vestal footsteps lightly tread,
And Cupids sport around the head,
   Of gentle Doctor Francis.[100]

While placed on high exalted pegs,
Apollo blushes for his legs,
   And mourns his severed fingers;
Some amorous wight, with passion drunk,
O'er Cythera's headless trunk,
   Luxuriously lingers.

Here Danæ rolls her humid eyes,
To meet the ruler of the skies,
   In tricks that please old Satan;
And there, our eyes delighted trace
The scarlet coat and lily face
   Of gallant Captain Creighton.[191]

Here West's creative pencil shines,[192]
And paints in tear-compelling lines,
   Polony's crazy daughter;
A hang-dog king, and sheepish queen,
And she — that looks as if she'd been
   Just fished up from the water.

Thy glories too are blazoned there
King Ben's first born immortal heir-
   Apparent to the pallet;
Orlando weighs his *cons* and *pros*,
Forgetting quite his heedless toes
   Are in the Phoca's gullet.

   *   *   *   *   *   *

> "*I can not but remember such things were,*
> *And were most pleasant to me.*"
>   Macbeth.

Oh! where are now the lights that shed
   A lustre on my darkened hours?
The priests of pleasure's fane, who spread
Each night, beneath my weary head,
   Endymion's moonlight couch of flowers.

No more in chains of music bound,
   I listen to those airy reels,
When quavering Philipps cuts around
Fantastic pigeon-wings of sound,
Like Byrne, who, without touching ground,
   Eleven times can cross his heels.

No longer Cooper's tongue of tongues,
Pumps thunder from his stormy lungs;
   Turner has shut his classic pages,
Southward his face Magenis turns,
And for the halls of Congress spurns
   The mansion of our civic sages.

By Robbins frighted from our coasts,
   My Potter, too, suspends his tricks,
While to amuse old Pluto's hosts,
Day Francis plays to grinning ghosts
   His juggles on the shores of Styx.

And Wallack [193] now no longer dips
   In bathos, for the tragic prize;
And Bartley's melalogue, that slips
Melodious from her honied lips,
   No more in murmured music dies.

Yet tho' fell fortune has bereft
My heart of all — one mode is left
   In slumber's vision to restore 'em:
Weekly, I'll buy with pious pence,
A dose of opiate eloquence,
   And sleep in quiet at the Forum.

TO QUACKERY.

Goddess! for such thou art, who rules
  This honest and enlightened city;
Thou patroness of knaves and fools,
  To thee we dedicate our ditty.
Whether in Barclay street thou sittest,
  Or, on papyrean pinions borne,
Dropping mercurial dews thou flittest
  Around thine own anointed Horne.[1]

Whether arrayed in gown and band
  Thy pious zeal distributes Bibles,
Or perched on Spooner's classic hand,
  Writes many eulogistic libels;
Where e'er we turn our raptured eyes
  We see this puffing generation,
Cheered by thy smile, propitious, rise
  To profit, power and reputation.

Then come ye quacks! the anthem swell,
    Come Allen with thy lottery bills,
Come four herb Angelis,[195] who fell
    From Heaven in a shower of pills.
Come Geib![196] whose potent word creates
    Prime analytical musicians,
And come ye hosts, that hold brevets
    From David's college of physicians.

And thou, botanic Hosack, bring
    Thy slander-breathing lips along;
Thy name, great charlatan, shall ring
    The monarch of the motley throng.
Yet Mitchill may the votes estrange,
    Or Doctor Clinton to confound ye,
Again produce some queer melange
    Of scientific Salmagundi.

Clinton! the name my fancy fires,
    I see him with a sage's look,
Exhausting nature and whole quires
    Of foolscap — in his wondrous book!
Columbia's genius hovers o'er him,
    Fair Science, smiling, lingers near,
Encyclopedias lie before him,
    And Mitchill whispers in his ear.

Enough! the swelling wave has borne
  Upon its bosom, chiefs and kings
From Mitchell—Clinton—Hosack—Horne—
  We can not stop to meaner things.
Yet once again, we'll raise the song
  And passing forums, banks and brokers,
Join with the bubble-blowing throng,
  Seize Quackery's pipe, and puff the Croakers.

THE MILITIA.

> "So some cock-sparrow in a farmer's yard,
> Hops at the head of a huge flock of turkeys."
> Tom Thumb.

Mr. Clinton, whose worth we shall know when we've lost him,
Is delightfully free of his gifts, if they cost him
  But little or nothing, like smiles and brevets.
With what wonderful *tact*, he appreciates merit
In bestowing on all our grown lads of spirit,
  His ensigns' commissions and gold epaulets.
'Tis amusing to see these young nurslings of fame,
With their flashes of crimson and collars of flame;
Their cock'd hats enchanting — their buttons divine;
And even the cloth of their coats — superfine!
Displaying, around us, their new tinsel riches,
  As proud as a boy in his first pair of breeches.

Ah! who does not envy their steps of delight
   Through the streets, at the side of their warriors prancing;
While, scared at their "chimney sweep badges," so bright
Cartmen, pigs and old women seek safety in flight,
   As, in exquisite order, their lines are advancing.
Long live the militia! from sergeant to drummer
   They've the true soldier-aspect, chivalric and wild,
In their clothes of more hues than the rainbow of summer,
   Or the coat which the patriarch wore when a child:
Unawed by *court-martials*, by fines, or by fears,
They glow with the feelings of free volunteers;
How *un*like British tars, with a rope's end held o'er 'em,
Their hands tied behind, and a pressgang before 'em!

Long live the militia! thou free school of glory!
   Mapes, Steddiford, Colden were nurtured by thee;
Lives there a man who ne'er heard their proud story,
   What an unlettered, ignorant dog he must be!
From the Battery flag-staff, their fame has ascended
   To the sand hills of Greenwich and plains of Bellevue;
And the belles of Park place for the palm have contended
   Of rewarding the feats they have promised to do.
Let the poets of Europe still scribble as hard as
   They please, of their Cæsars and Bonys to tell,
Be ours the bright names of Laight, Ward and Bogardus,
   And that promising genius, the brave Colonel Pell.

NOTES.

NOTES.

1. Doctor LANGSTAFF, an Apothecary in this city, and by many reputed the discoverer of pure magnesium at Hoboken.

2. MORDECAI MANNASSAH NOAH was born in Philadelphia in 1785, where he studied law, and mingled in politics and literature. In 1813, President Madison appointed him United States Consul to Morocco. He returned to America in 1819, and published a volume of his travels, and established himself at New York, where he edited the *National Advocate*. In 1820, he formed a project of collecting the Jews upon Grand Island in the Niagara river, but this, like all previous attempts to gather this people, proved abortive. In his memorial to the Legislature for the purchase of the Island, he asked for a law giving sanction to the measure, to remove any doubts his coreligionists might have about removing from the old world with the certainty of finding an asylum in the new. A monument was erected on the Island to commemorate the attempt, and upon a marble tablet was inscribed the following inscription:

שבע שראלדר אלהרנר
רראהר

ARARAT.
A CITY OF REFUGE FOR THE JEWS.

Founded by MORDECAI M. NOAH, in the month of Tizri, 5586 (September, 1825), and in the 50th year of American Independence.

In 1821, he was appointed Sheriff of New York by the Council of Appointment. He was afterwards connected with the *New York Enquirer* and the *Evening Star*, and established the *Sunday Times*, with which paper he continued until his death on the 22d March, 1851. No man in the city was better known than Major Noah, and no man possessed a greater fund of anecdote, or acquaintance with public characters, with whom his newspaper undertakings had brought him in contact.—*Ency. of Am. Literature.*

3. Lady Morgan's clever book on France had been recently published.

4. *Altorf*, a tragedy, by Frances Wright, performed at the Park Theatre. It enjoyed but a brief existence, although it had the benefit of an excellent cast of characters, including Wallack, Pritchard, Mrs. Barnes and others. It was first performed on the 19th February, 1819. The play was published by Carey & Son of Philadelphia.

5. MICAH HAWKINS wrote a play called *The Sawmill, or a Yankee Trick*, which was performed at Barriere's Chatham Theatre, in Chatham street, below Pearl street.

6. ALDEN SPOONER was the publisher of the *New York Columbian*, and subsequently of the *Long Island Star*.

7. The firm of Sturges & Crowninshield, received a discharge under the insolvent law of this state in 1811. The contract which formed the basis of this suit, was made before the passing of this law. The Supreme Court of the United States (Chief Justice Marshall) decided: That a bankrupt law is not necessarily such a law as discharges the debt, and, therefore, until Congress shall exercise the power contained in the Constitution, by passing a national bankrupt law, the states may pass bankrupt laws provided they be not such laws as impair the obligation of contracts. "They may discharge the person of an insolvent trader from liability to imprisonment, but they can not pass a law annulling the contract, or discharging the liability of future acquisitions."—*N. Y. Columbian, March*, 1819.

8. CHARLES N. BALDWIN published the *Republican Chronicle* in this city, which was discontinued on the 6th March, 1819, and the subscription list transferred to the *Columbian*.

9. This famous box is described as of plain gold, with a chased rim. It bears the following inscription: "Presented by the Mayor, Aldermen and Commonalty of the City of New York, to Maj'r. Gen. Andrew Jackson, with the freedom of the city, as a testimony of respect for his high military service." The presentation took place on the 23d Feb. 1819, the address being made by the Mayor, Cadwallader

D. Colden. General Jackson retained the box till his death in June, 1845, when the following disposition of it was found in his last will and testament, dated 7th June, 1843.

"The gold box presented to me by the Corporation of the City of New York, the large silver vase presented to me by the ladies of Charleston, South Carolina, my native state, with the large picture representing the unfurling of the American banner, presented to me by the citizens of South Carolina when it was refused to be accepted by the United States Senate, I leave in trust to my son A. Jackson jr., with directions that should our happy country not be blessed with peace, an event not always to be expected, he will, at the close of the war, or end of the conflict, present each of said articles of inestimable value, to that patriot residing in the city or state from which they were presented, who shall be adjudged by his countrymen or the ladies, to have been the most valiant in defence of his country and our country's rights."

The enlistment of New York Volunteers in the Mexican war, which ended with the capitulation of Mexico, gave an opportunity for the executor of the will, Andrew Jackson, the son of the testator, to discharge the trust. In 1857, he was in correspondence with the Common Council of New York, and arrangements were made, which promised the delivery of the box to Lt. Col. Garret Dyckman, of the regiment of Volunteers. A committee of the Volunteers had arranged a military parade for the occasion; Mr. Jackson was in the city with the box in his possession, when, at the last moment, he sent, in a letter, his "regret at the division of sentiment and the excited feelings" which had come to his knowledge with reference to the disposal of the box, which he bore away with him to be kept for a clearer expression of public opinion. In 1859, it was finally awarded to Gen. Ward B. Burnett, the Colonel of the New York regiment which participated in the brilliant operations at Vera Cruz, Cerro Gordo, Contreras and Cherubusco. The presentation was made at the City Hall, Nashville, Tenn. Dr. John M. Lawrence for his father-in-law, Andrew Jackson, the executor, and General Pillow receiving the bequest in behalf of General Burnett, who was unavoidably absent on a western government exploration. Thus ends the present history of the Jackson snuff-box, inaugurated by Drake in the *Croakers*.

10. BARTHOLOMEW SKAATS, or *Barty Skaats*, as he was familiarly called, was for many years Crier of the Courts, which were held in the old City Hall in Wall street. Both he and his wife are identified with the past history of the city. They were excellent personifications of

respectable Dutch character, in dress, in habits, in hospitality, in prudence and industry. The good cheer and excellent hospitality of this worthy couple, led to the establishment of the *Tea Room*, for many years so celebrated. When the present City Hall was finished, Mr. and Mrs. Skaats removed to it as keepers. Soon afterwards a suggestion was made to them to establish in their rooms, a regular table for the Common Council and its guests, and to attend to it, at the expense of the Corporation. Mr. Skaats being *well-to-do* in the world, indignantly declined the proposition, and resigned his situation as keeper, and Abraham Martling, the keeper of Tammany Hall, succeeded him.—*Corporation Manual.*

11. A grand dinner was given to General Jackson at Tammany Hall, on the 23d Feb. 1819, in honor of his visit to this city. The hall was crowded, and the toast "To General Jackson, so long as the Mississippi rolls its waters to the ocean, so long may his great name and glorious deeds be remembered," was replied to by the General, who proposed "De Witt Clinton, Governor of the great and patriotic State of New York," to the utter confusion of the Bucktails, who looked upon Clinton as their bitterest foe. General Jackson, perfectly independent of all parties, had conceived a great admiration for Mr. Clinton, although he was, at that time, personally unacquainted with him, and hence the toast. The greatest confusion ensued, amid which the General left the room.

12. MEAD and HAWKINS were destitute of voice, and those who knew their want of ability, could appreciate the satire in this line.

13. JOHN P. HAFF, Sachem of the Tammany Society, and afterwards Surveyor of the Port of New York.

14. ABRAHAM BLOODGOOD, a leading man at Tammany Hall.

15. CADWALLADER D. COLDEN succeeded De Witt Clinton as Mayor of New York in 1818, and was afterwards elected to Congress, and to the State Senate. He bestowed much attention in devising the means of promoting, in various ways, the improvement of the community to which he belonged. The public schools of New York and the Society for the Reformation of Juvenile Delinquents especially ranked him among their most efficient patrons. He was one of the earliest and most zealous promoters of the system of internal improvements in the state. In the history of the Erie canal, his name is often mentioned in

connection with measures conducive to the accomplishment of that work; the *Memoir* of which, by him, was printed by the Common Council of this city. He died at Jersey City on the 7th of February, 1834.

16. Gen. ROBERT BOGARDUS was for nearly fifty years a member of the New York bar. He was a member of the State Senate from 1827 to 1829 inclusive, and for many years an active member of the New York militia, having with Cadwallader D. Colden received the appointment of brevet Brigadier-General from Gov. Clinton. He died in this city on the 12th September, 1842.

17. DENNIS H. DOYLE, an Irishman, who from humble beginnings accumulated a fortune, and retired to Ulster county, where he died.

18. GURDON S. MUMFORD, a merchant of this city, and during six years a member of Congress.

19. Doctor BRONAUGH, a Military Surgeon, "was attached to Gen. Jackson's staff during the whole Seminole campaign," and was a strong personal friend of Jackson.

20. In the *Assembly Journal* of this year, under date Sept. 8th, there appears a resolution offered by Gen. Root, which passed, calling on Gov. Clinton for a list of his brevet appointments. The Governor sent it in, amounting to nineteen brevet Major Generals, thirteen Brigadiers and sixty-six other military officers.—*Assembly Journal*, 1819.

21. The late Major Gen. MORTON, who was in command of the militia in this district at the time, and in which he continued until his death. He also held the office of Clerk to the Common Council for twenty-six years, and died while still an incumbent of that office in December 1836, at an age exceeding eighty years.

23. Doctor CHARLES KING, now President of Columbia College in this city.

24. FERRIS PELL wrote a defense of Clinton's administration, entitled *A Review of the Administration and Civil Police of the State of New York from* 1807 *to* 1819.

25. WILLIAM BAYARD was one of the firm of Le Roy, Bayard & McEvers, prominent merchants of New York, and nearly related, by marriage, to General Stephen Van Rensselaer of Albany.

26. SAMUEL SWARTWOUT was for many years connected with public life in this country. In his youth, he became personally attached to the late Col. Burr, and the friendship continued until his death. General Jackson appointed Mr. Swartwout Collector of the Port of New York, which office he held until he was detected in serious defalcations, upon which he left for Europe, where he remained for two years, and then returned to this city. He resided here until his death in November 1856. In 1814, Messrs. Samuel and Robert Swartwout purchased 4000 acres of land at Hoboken, New Jersey. It was at that time sunken, spongy and uncongenial to vegetation, being subject to the constant overflowing of the tide waters. They immediately commenced to reclaim the land by erecting permanent dikes and opening ditches. By the year 1819, they had made seven and a half miles of embankment, and one hundred and twenty miles of ditches. Two thousand acres were enclosed by dikes and thirteen hundred acres completely drained and under successful cultivation. About one hundred cows were in this year fed upon these reclaimed marshes, and their milk sent to the New York market. Grain of various kinds and vegetables in abundance were also raised. The funds of the proprietors appear to have now run out, for in 1819 they applied to the Corporation of New York for aid to complete their work. The application was not successful and the project was abandoned.—*Eve. Post, July* 24, 1819.

27. Mr. POTTER gave exhibitions in ventriloquism in Washington Hall in Broadway, where Stewart's store now stands.

28. LEVI ROBBINS was, in 1819, a member of Assembly from Lewis county. He took a leading part in the first temperance movement in that section of the state, and as a town officer instituted several suits against persons for violating the excise law then existing. These proceedings excited much discussion among his fellow townsmen, and his course was warmly defended or opposed, according to the instincts of each. He is still living—the perfect model of a Baptist deacon, his face still set against sin in every form, and we will venture to say, as ready now to promote as he was then to present any document kindred to the "memorial of a convention of delegates from the several moral societies within this state, praying for the enaction of certain

legal provisions for the suppression of vice and immorality," which was offered by him about this time. The journals do not show that a bill was actually introduced, and the occasion which prompted this poem proved a *false alarm.*

29. ERASTUS ROOT made his first appearance in public life in the State Assembly in the year 1798. He continued for many years in the Legislature, and though somewhat uncouth and rough in his manners, and occasionally rude in his expressions, his wit was keen, and his sarcasm severe and biting. He seized with great effect upon the prominent points, and especially those points most likely to make an impression upon the public ear, and pressed them with a power almost irresistible. His illustrations were exceedingly clear and well chosen, and his attacks upon his opponents were severe almost to ferocity. His attacks upon De Witt Clinton and his canal policy were especially marked. He was perfectly at home on all matters relating to the history of the operations of both great political parties. He had much parliamentary tact, and although he was reckless in his expressions, he was a man of correct literary taste, and though irregular in his habits, of highly cultivated intellect.—*Hammond's Political History.*

30. ABRAHAM MARTLING kept a tavern on the corner of Nassau and Spruce streets, and afterwards became Proprietor of Tammany Hall. On the resignation of Mr. Skaats, he was appointed Keeper of the City Hall.

31. PETER SHARPE, a member of the Assembly from the city of New York in 1815, and from 1817 to 1821 inclusive. He was Speaker of the Assembly in the latter year.

32. OBADIAH GERMAN of Chenango county, made his first appearance in public life in 1798 in the Assembly of this State. Although uneducated, he was a bold and resolute man, of great intellectual strength and vigor. He acquired great influence in the Legislature of the State, and in 1809 was elected Senator of the United States, as the successor of Doctor Mitchill. In 1818, he was again elected to the Assembly of the State, and was made Speaker of the House.—*Hammond.*

33. EZEKIEL BACON, late Comptroller of the United States Treasury, a Clintonian member from Oneida and Oswego counties, was a man of considerable talent, but the strength and vigor of his mind had been greatly impaired by a nervous disease. He now resides in Utica at an advanced age.—*Hammond.*

34. Mr. SYLVANUS MILLER was appointed Surrogate of New York in 1801. At the time of his appointment, he was a resident of Ulster county, and the New York people complained of the Council, for importing a Surrogate from the country. He was the ardent friend of De Witt Clinton, and always continued his unwavering supporter. The good nature and prepossessing deportment of Mr. Miller soon gained him the good will of the New Yorkers. Possessed of fine conversational powers, and ready wit, which was dealt out in such a manner as never to wound the feelings of others, and of a disposition the most social, he soon became the favorite of all who knew him. He held the office of Surrogate, which in the great city of New York is a highly important one, from August, 1801, till February, 1821, with an interval of one year. He is still living in this city at a very advanced age.—*Hammond.*

35. The corner stone of the Park Theatre was laid in 1795, but, owing to a quarrel between the managers, Hallam and Hodgkinson, was not completed until 1798. Mr. Dunlap shortly after undertook the management, which he continued until 1808, when it passed into the hands of Messrs. Cooper and Price. When Mr. Cooper retired, Mr. Simpson became associated with Mr. Price. During their management, it was burned (in 1821), but was immediately rebuilt, and opened for dramatic representation on the 1st September of the same year. Mr. Price died in 1840, and Mr. Simpson assumed the sole direction of the establishment, which he continued until 1848, when owing to his misfortunes, it passed into the hands of Mr. Thomas S. Hamblin, and in December of that year it was again destroyed by fire, and not rebuilt. It is generally supposed that the loss of the lease of the theatre was the proximate cause of Mr. Simpson's death, which took place shortly after Mr. Hamblin obtained the lease. Twice, whilst he was in the management of the theatre, he might have retired with a large fortune; but his love of the profession, and the entreaties of friendship, induced him to suffer the golden opportunities to pass by. As a manager, he was dignified, able and untiring. He possessed a refined taste, and was familiar with every thing connected with the drama and dramatic literature.—*N. Y. Atlas.*

36. SAMUEL WOODWORTH, the son of a Massachusetts farmer, was born in 1785. He was apprenticed to a printer in Boston, and after the expiration of his indentures, he removed to New Haven, and commenced a paper called the *Belles Lettres Repository*, of which he was "editor, publisher, printer, and sometimes carrier." It was discon-

tinued after a month or two. Mr. Woodworth afterwards came to this city, but was equally unsuccessful with the periodicals he commenced here. The *New York Mirror* was undertaken by him in connection with Gen. Morris, but at the end of a year Mr. Woodworth left. He worked at his trade, and occasionally contributed verses and patriotic songs to the periodicals of the day, and wrote a play called the *Forest Rose* which was performed at the old Chatham Theatre, and still keeps possession of the stage. In his latter years he suffered from paralysis, and died on the 9th December, 1842.—*Ency. of Am. Lit.*

37. Mr. WILLIAM COLEMAN came to this city from Massachusetts, and established the *Evening Post* in 1801. "He was a sensitive man, of great tenacity of opinion, which he cherished by intercourse with many of the leading patriots and politicians who were among us some fifty years ago." He continued the sole editor of the paper until 1819, when his health was seriously affected by a paralytic attack, and it became necessary for him to have a coadjutor in his labors. His connection with the paper continued until his death, which took place in the summer of 1819.

38. Miss CATHARINE LEESUGG made her first appearance in New York Sept. 1st, 1818, in the characters of Jessy Oatland and Marian Ramsay. She possessed a buxom figure, a clear, melodious voice, great sprightliness and vivacity, and won her way at once to public favor. Her *forte* was comedy; her merry country lasses have not since been equaled, and although she sometimes played tragic parts, she was not so happy in them. In 1819, while in the height of her popularity, she married Mr. James Hackett, and left the stage. She resumed the profession in 1826, and was for several years afterwards one of the favorites of the town. Her last appearance was for her husband's benefit at the National Theatre, in Leonard street, on the 19th May, 1838. She died at her residence, Jamaica, L. I., December 4th, 1845, aged 47 years.—*Playgoers' Journal.*

39. Mr. HOPPER, a native of this city, was attached to the Park Theatre during the year 1819, and played minor parts. He remained but a short time upon the boards.

40. ROBERT CAMPBELL MAYWOOD made his first appearance in New York in January, 1819, as Richard III. He played the usual round of characters in tragedy and melo-drama, and gave general satisfaction.

His Sir Pertinax McSycophant is said never to have been equaled on the American stage, except by Cooke. Mr. Maywood remained in New York about ten years, and afterwards managed the theatres in Philadelphia and Baltimore. His last appearance in this city was in 1845 at the Olympic Theatre in Broadway. He died within the last three years in very reduced circumstances.

41. The Declaration of Independence.

42. Col. JOHN TRUMBULL of New Haven, Conn., died in New York on the 10th November, 1843, aged 87 years. He was born at Lebanon, Ct., June 9th, 1756. His father, Jonathan Trumbull, was Governor of Connecticut, during the whole war of the revolution. At an early age, John Trumbull entered the revolutionary army, and after serving with his regiment in the field, became a member of Gen. Washington's military family. During the revolution, he went to Europe, to perfect himself in his favorite art of painting, having it always at heart to perpetuate on canvas some of the great scenes and great men of the revolution. Four of his historical paintings, the Declaration of Independence, the Surrender at Saratoga, the Surrender of Cornwallis, and the Resignation of Gen. Washington at Annapolis, are preserved in the rotunda of the Capitol at Washington, and although they are not marked by the highest qualities of genius, they do honor to his reputation as an artist. While in England he became, by the choice of William Pinckney and Christopher Gore, the fifth commissioner under the Jay treaty, for the settlement of American claims upon England; and holding, as he did, the determining vote on all contested cases, he was so fortunate as to acquire the entire respect and confidence of both parties, by the strict impartiality and justice of his decisions. As a soldier, an artist, a diplomatist, and a gentleman, he was honored and beloved through several generations.—*Am. Almanac.*

43. Mr. JACOB SHERRED, a Painter and Glazier, accumulated a large property by his business, which he conducted in Broad street in this city. An obituary notice of him in the *Evening Post* of 30th March, 1821, says: "He closed a life of usefulness and benevolence, in a manner worthy of the brightness of its course. The greater part of his large fortune was bequeathed to the Protestant Episcopal Theological School in the State of New York."

44. A general meeting of the citizens was called at Washington Hall, to protest against taxing the property of the citizens generally, instead of those more nearly interested in the improvement of enlarging the Battery. This meeting was held on the 2d March, 1819, and a second meeting was held on the 12th of the same month, to hear the report of a committee upon the subject. The *Evening Post* of the 15th March, says:

"General Bogardus, chairman of a committee of seven, appointed at a previous meeting, read a long and tedious memorial to the Legislature against the contemplated improvements, and Mr. Thomas R. Mercein, who was one of the minority, then read a well drawn up protest against it. Several persons tried to address the meeting, but so numerous was the collection, and so great the clamor, that nothing could be heard but "question, question." The chairman then put it on the acceptance of the report of the committee, and all accounts agree that there was a majority of two to one, or three to two against it. The chairman however, being himself in favor of the report, declined to declare it, on which there was a call for a division of the house, but the crowd was so great, this was difficult to be accomplished, and after an ineffectual attempt by Gen. Bogardus to obtain an adjournment, the chairman abdicated the chair, and he and the general left the room. Col. Murray was then called to the chair, but he made a short speech, and advised the people to go home, as the object of the meeting was defeated. Thus has ended this attempt of certain men to array the people against the constituted authorities of the city; and it is strongly believed, they were secretly influenced by political motives, and intended to make what they thought would be a very popular measure, subservient to party views at the ensuing election. If so, it may literally be said "they counted without their *host*."

45. Washington Hall stood on the south-east corner of Broadway and Reade street. It was built by the Washington Benevolent Society in 1809, and was the head-quarters of the Federalists in this city, until their dissolution as a party. The building was afterwards sold to Mr. John G. Costar, and it was kept as a hotel until the year 1844, when on the 4th of July of that year, it was burned down, and Mr. A. T. Stewart became the purchaser. It now forms a portion of the store occupied by that gentleman.

46. LEWIS HARTMAN, Esq., presided at the meeting, and Mr. CHAS. KING was Secretary.

47. Col. Thomas R. Mercein was a member of the Legislature from this city in 1811 and 1812, and was distinguished for his activity and usefulness as a citizen. He died 24th October, 1843.—*Am. Almanac.*

48. James Lent was Register of the city and county of New York.

49. Mr. N. Prime, of the firm of Prime, Ward & King. Bankers in Wall street.

50. While no person became a more marked object of satire in these poems than Governor Clinton, it is proper to remark that no one enjoyed the *Croakers* more than he did.

51. This, we understand, is a typographical error; it should be paramount obligation.—*Ed. Eve. Post.*

52. We believe this is a mistake of the poet's. Mr. H. was commercial agent at Havana.—*Ed. Eve. Post.*

53. We understand that this declaration as to J. A. H., was gratuitously made. The political opinions of these two gentlemen have differed very widely for the last four or five years.—*Ed. Eve. Post.*

54. This poem, as printed in the *Evening Post*, was prefixed with the following lines written by Mr. Coleman:
"Sage of Plandome! to give thy due,
Fredonian, Frede and Fredon" too—

55. The name given by our learned philosopher to the steam ship upon her being launched during the late war.—*Ed. Eve. Post.*

56. Mummy-chogs, the popular name of the *fundulus*, a common fish in the bays near New York.

56. Referring to the work entitled *Lives and Portraits of Distinguished Americans*, by Joseph Delaplaine, Philadelphia, 1816-18, 2 vols. 4to.

57. John Minshull, an Englishman by birth, was a butt of the critics of his day. He wrote and published, "printed for the author," *Rural Felicity*, an opera; a comedy, entitled, *The Sprightly Widow in*

the Frolics of Youth; or a speedy way of uniting the Sexes by Honorable Marriage, New York, 1803; *He Stoops to Conquer, or the Virgin Wife Triumphant*; a comedy in three acts, New York 1804; *The Merry Dames, or the Humourist's Triumph over the Poet in Petticoats, and the Gallant Exploits of the Knight of the Comb*, New York, 1805. Minshull's plays were performed at the Park Theatre. The wits humoured his jokes by loud applause, and called on him for a speech from the stage box. His portrait, engraved by Scoles, ruffled and queued, a sprightly, perked-up physiognomy, is prefixed to the edition of his plays; his coat of arms with a crescent, and the motto *In hoc plenius redibo*, figures beneath, with the motto:

> Next view and peruse my plan,
> Refrain from laughing who can.

58. JAMES K. PAULDING.

> So have I seen in garden rich and gay,
> A stately cabbage waxing fat each day;
> Unlike the lively foliage of the trees,
> Its stubborn leaves ne'er wave in summer breeze,
> Nor flower, like those that prank the walks around,
> Upon its clumsy stem is ever found;
> It heeds not noontide heats, or evening's balm,
> And stands unmov'd in one eternal calm.
> At last, when all the garden's pride is lost,
> It ripens in drear autumn's killing frost,
> And in a sav'ry sourkrout finds its end,
> From which detested dish, me Heaven defend!
> *Backwoodsman*, Book II.

59. HENRY MEIGS, of New York city, represented the Second Congressional District in the sixteenth Congress, 1819-1821.

60. The tragedy of *Brutus* has been censured for want of originality, which the writer acknowledges, by admitting that he borrowed the ideas and occasionally the words of others, but a great proof of its merit is that it is the only one of eight plays upon the same subject that keeps possession of the stage.—*Playgoers' Journal*.

61. THOMAS KILNER made his first appearance at the Park Theatre in December, 1818, as Sir Abel Handy, and soon proved himself a valuable acquisition to the company. He played principally in old men, and whether serious or comic, seldom failed to represent them to

the satisfaction of the audience. He afterwards went to Boston, where he was manager of the theatre, and last played in New York, at the Bowery Theatre, in 1837. He finally removed to Ohio, where he was living in 1855.—*Playgoers' Journal.*

62. HARRY GEORGE MORELAND was from the York Theatre, and was a useful and available actor. He was a pleasing singer, a correct reader, and as an actor in the lighter characters of the drama always gave satisfaction. He died in New York, 13th June, 1832.

63. On the 2d Sept., 1818, Mr. James Howard, from the Brighton Theatre, made his first appearance as Henry Bertram. He had a sweet tenor voice, a good face and figure, and as a vocalist for several years enjoyed the highest favor. He last played at the Park Theatre, in 1828, and in 1837 appeared for the last time in New York, at Niblo's Garden, on crutches, having had one or both legs fractured during his retirement. He died in Philadelphia in 1848.

64. Mr. GARNER appeared on the 3d Sept. 1818, and was a valuable acquisition for the lighter operatic parts. He afterwards played at the Lafayette Theatre in Laurens street in 1828, and died in Baltimore 1843.—*Playgoers' Journal.*

65. The following letter addressed to *the Editor*, was written by Mr. Coleman, and prefixed to the poem to John Lang:

"Monday evening — 9 o'clock.
"Mr. Editor.

"As soon as it was dark I repaired to the usual place, and there found your note inclosing the lines alluded to in this evening's paper, on the subject of Mr. Lang, who in Saturday morning's Gazette, pretends that he had received a 'poetic effusion,' as he calls it, from us, and which he said was too personal for his paper. Personalities are become quite alarming to Mr. Lang ever since the suit of Jacob Barker for what he said of the *red notes.* However, the purpose of this is to convince Mr. Lang that I have been among the most attentive of his readers and admirers for years; with delight have I enjoyed his well-turned paragraphs, and his witty expressions, some of which could not escape my memory. Like Falstaff 'he is not only witty himself, but the cause of wit in others.' So here we go." In the *New York Gazette* of 20th March, 1819, appears the following: "The poetic effusion of Croaker & Co. is too personal for this Gazette."

66. Mr. JOHN LANG was born in the city of New York, in 1770. For forty years he conducted the *New York Gazette*, which was recognized as the leading commercial paper. Its distinction was unquestionably its attention to the shipping interests of this city, for in political or miscellaneous matter, it was sadly deficient. Lang's prominent object of consideration was *arrivals*, and the mightiest changes of revolutions, in actions or opinions, found but a passing notice in his paper. But from the support of the mercantile community, the paper flourished, and Mr. Lang became rich. He was devoted to his pursuits, and no one could excel him in kindness of demeanor. He was a gentleman of the old school, of great moral excellence, and deeply devoted to the interests of the city. He died in the year 1836.

67. Lang's Bulletins, with an allusion to his popular name of *Solomon*, figure in the education of Fanny's father, in Halleck's poem *Fanny*. Then in Pearl street

                    "first he met
The Editor of the New York Gazette,

"The sapient Mr. Lang. The world of him
   Knows much, yet not one-half so much as he
Knows of the world. Up to its very brim
   The goblet of his mind is sparkling free
With lore and learning. Had proud Sheba's queen,
In all her bloom and beauty, but have seen

"This modern Solomon, the Israelite,
   Earth's monarch as he was, had never won her.
He would have hanged himself for very spite,
   And she, blessed woman, might have had the honor
Of some neat *paragraphs* — worth all the lays
That Judah's minstrel warbled in her praise.

"Her star arose too soon; but that which swayed
   Th' ascendant at our merchant's natal hour
Was bright with better destiny — its aid
   Led him to pluck, within the classic bower
Of bulletins, the blossoms of true knowledge;
And Lang supplied the loss of school and college."

68. The office of the *New York Gazette* was in Hanover square, between Hanover and Pearl streets. The bust of Franklin which formerly surmounted the roof of the building, is now in possession of the New York Historical Society.

69. In the year 1814, a writer appeared in a New York paper assuming the name of Abimelech Coody, a mechanic of that place. He was a Federalist, and addressed himself principally to the party to which he belonged. He endeavored to show the impropriety of opposing the war, and urged them to come forward manfully in defence of their country. The writer was soon ascertained to be Mr. Gulian C. Verplanck. Abimelech Coody was replied to by a writer, over the signature of A Traveller with great point and severity, who was said to be De Witt Clinton, who said that "he [Coody alias Verplanck,] has become the head of a sect called the *Coodies*, of hybrid nature, composed of the combined spawn of Federalism and Jacobinism, without any definite character; neither fish nor flesh, nor bird nor beast, but a nondescript made up of

'All monstrous, all prodigous things.'"

The result of the next election in April, 1815, proved that they made no impression on the Federal party in New York, for from being Democratic in 1814, the city changed to Federalism in 1815.—*Hammond*.

70. There was an order of the Tammany Society, who wore in their hats as an insignia, on certain occasions, a portion of the tail of a deer. They were a leading order, and from this circumstance, the friends of Mr. Clinton gave those who adopted the views of the members of the Tammany Society in relation to him, the name of *Bucktails;* which name was eventually applied to their friends and supporters in the country. Hence, the party opposed to the administration of Mr. Clinton was, for a long time, called the *Bucktail Party.*—*Hammond*.

71. John Wesley Jarvis was for many years the most eminent portrait painter in New York. He was born in England, and came to this country when quite a child. He studied engraving under Edwin, and commenced painting in 1806, and soon reached the head of the profession. Two of his full-lengths, Gen. Brown and Com. Bainbridge, are now in the City Hall. He was an inimitable story-teller, but his irregular habits of living caused a gradual decay of his powers as a painter. He died in this city on the 12th January, 1841.—*Arts of Design*.

NOTES.

72. DOMINICK LYNCH, jr., a Merchant of this city, to whose exertions the American public were indebted for the introduction of Italian opera in this country. The troupe led by Garcia arrived in November 1825, and appeared at the Park theatre shortly afterwards.

73. Mr. T. PHILIPPS made two visits to this country. The first in 1815, when he made his *début* as Count Belino, in the *Devil's Bridge*, and at once attained the highest summit of popular favor. He had a fine personal appearance, his voice was unrivaled for sweetness, and he sung with more feeling and expression than any other vocalist who had been heard here, Incledon only excepted. Mr. Coleman, of the *Evening Post*, praised him extravagantly, and said of his singing that "you could hear the poet as well as the musician." His second visit was in 1822 and 1823, when he made his last appearance in June of the latter year.—*Playgoers' Journal*.

74. On the 22d April, 1815, Mr. JOHN BARNES made his first appearance in America as Sir Peter Teazle and Lingo. He soon became an immense favorite, and probably caused more laughter than any comedian we have ever had. The comical phiz of *Old Barnes* was always the signal for a burst of merriment, and they who censured his numerous extravagances were obliged to laugh at his whimsical grimaces. He left the Park Theatre in 1832, and undertook the management of the Richmond Hill Theatre, in Varick street, which proved an unfortunate speculation. He occasionally afterwards appeared at the Park, where he played for the last time in 1840. While on a professional visit to Nova Scotia, in 1841, he was taken ill, and died on the 28th August, aged 60 years. His remains were brought to New York, and interred in St. Mark's burying ground.—*Playgoers' Journal*.

75. The poet is supposed to intend a hit at Mr. Duff, one of the Boston managers, who, with about as much pretensions to it as the actor here named, actually went all the way to Philadelphia, a few weeks since, to personate Count Belino; but having, by the assistance of numerous orders, murdered it for two nights, poor Wood flinched from any farther experiment. They manage these things better in Boston. Here they have an ingenious contrivance by which they suit the play to the man, whenever the man is not suited to the play; thus on a late occasion, in order to enable a modest young Irishman, by the name of Keene, to sustain the character of Belino, they cut the *Devil's Bridge* down to a farce.—*Ed. Eve. Post*.

76. Mr. Beekman, one of the owners of the Park Theatre.

77. The Franklin Bank occupied the building in Franklin square, on the corner of Cherry street, which was built by Walter Franklin, and occupied by Gen. Washington during the first year of his presidency. After the failure of the bank, the building was altered and Messrs. Firth & Hall occupied it as a music store until it was removed in 1856 to make room for the New Bowery extension.

78. The Surgeon's Hall was in Barclay street, at Nos. 9 and 11, near Broadway, and was pulled down in 1855.

79. Governor Tompkins's residence was on Staten Island between the Quarantine and New Brighton, directly fronting this city.

80. The North Dutch Church, the only one in Albany which could then boast of two steeples.

81. The Tammany Society or Columbian Order, was formed by William Mooney, an upholsterer, residing in New York during the administration of President Washington. It takes its name from the celebrated Indian chief, Tammany, whose attachment to liberty was greater than his love of life. It has a Grand Sachem, and thirteen Sachems, in imitation of the President and Governors of the States, and a Grand Council, of which the Sachems are members. Tammany was, at first, so popular, that most persons of merit became members; and so numerous were they that its anniversary (12th of May) was regarded as a holiday. At that time, there were no party politics mixed up in its proceedings. But when President Washington rebuked "self-created societies," from an apprehension that their ultimate tendency would be hostile to the public tranquility, the members of Tammany, supposing their institution to be included in the reproof, nearly all left it. The founder (Grand Sachem Mooney) and a few others continued steadfast, and from this time it became a political institution, and took ground with Jefferson. It continued to increase in members, and made a great rally about 1812 in support of President Madison's administration, and to secure his reëlection in that year. The society has been continued to the present time, solely as a political organization.—*Hammond.*

82. John P. Haff, afterward Surveyor of the Port of New York.

83. BENJAMIN BAILEY, a Merchant of this city, of the firm of Bailey & Bogart, an active politician, and for several years, Chairman of the Democratic General Committee at Tammany Hall.

84. CHARLES CHRISTIAN, a Justice of the Peace.

85. JOSEPH W. BRACKET, a Lawyer of this city.

86. Col. EVERARDUS WARNER, a Justice of the Police.

87. Gen. JONAS MAPES, a very worthy citizen, who held a commission as Major General of the Militia in this district, and also filled several offices of trust and honor in this city.

88. The Tammany Society had for several years but very indifferent quarters at Martling's Long Room, on the corner of Nassau and Spruce streets, where the Tract House now stands. In the year 1809, they determined to provide better accommodations, and passed a "Law" for the "Building of a Wigwam," of which the following is the preamble: "Whereas, several members of Tammany Society, or Columbian Order, have voluntary offered to subscribe moneys for the purchase of ground and the erection of a Wigwam for the use of this institution, and the general accommodation of Republicans," &c., &c. A committee of thirteen, corresponding with the number of the original states, was appointed to carry the *law* into effect. The sole survivor of this committee is Jacob Barker, now of New Orleans. The committee purchased a site on the corner of Chatham and Frankfort streets, and on the 13th May, 1811, the 22d anniversary of the Society, the corner stone was laid with great ceremony by the Grand Sachem, Clarkson Crolius, and an oration was delivered by Alpheus Sherman. The building was finished in the following year, and has continued to the present time to be the rallying point of the Democracy.

89. Doctor SAMUEL L. MITCHILL was appointed Surgeon General of the State of New York by Governor Clinton, being the first person who held that office. His report fills eight folio pages of the Senate journal.

90. Mr. COLEMAN altered the first line of this poem to—

"Ah! Julia! no more at each party and ball,"

as he considered the name of Chloe too antiquated.

91. On the south-east corner of William and Pine streets (originally called Smith and King streets) stood the family mansion of the Philipses. It was during the latter part of the last century kept as a lodging house by a Mrs. Mercer; then it passed into the hands of a Mr. King, and finally into the possession of his son-in-law, William Niblo, under whose charge it became famous as the Bank Coffee House. Mr. Niblo entered the service of Mr. King in an humble capacity, but by his attention to the interest of his employer, he was gradually advanced in position; in 1819 he married the daughter of Mr. King, and became proprietor of the establishment. He continued there until he took charge of the present Niblo's Garden, with which he is still connected.

92. Few actresses have been so deserving, fewer still have been so fortunate, as Mrs. BARNES, who made her first appearance at the Park Theatre, on the 17th April, 1815. During a theatrical career of twenty-five years, nothing occurred to detract in the slightest degree from the kindly feelings entertained for her, on her first appearance. In person, Mrs. Barnes was finely formed, and her features, though small, were eminently beautiful, and at her perfect command in portraying every shade of passion. She excelled principally in the youthful heroines of tragedy, though she was almost equally successful in comedy, melodrama and pantomime. Mrs. Barnes was respected and admired in private life, and after her husband's death, took a formal farewell of the stage November 2d, 1841. She has appeared a few times since for the benefit of her daughter, Miss Charlotte Barnes; the last occasion having been in Philadelphia, as Lady Randolph, on the 25th July, 1851, which character she sustained with almost undiminished excellence.—*Playgoers' Journal.*

93. The name of STEPHEN PRICE, so well known in theatrical annals, occurs in connection with the management of the Park Theatre for the first time in the year 1808, he having then purchased an interest of Mr. Cooper. His interest continued for thirty-two years, a portion of the time being with Mr. Simpson. Mr. Price was a man of great perseverance and energy of character, strict and severe, though honorable in his dealings, and displayed great taste and judgment in all his dramatic engagements. A long residence abroad, during which he was for a time manager of Drury Lane Theatre in London, gave him great facilities for the engagement of distinguished talent, and through him many of the most eminent British artists were introduced to the

American public. During the last years of Mr. Price's management, owing to the powerful rivalry of Mr. Wallack at the National Theatre in Leonard street, the Park Theatre declined greatly in popularity, and Mr. Price being absent could not understand the necessity of new outlays, which were necessary to keep pace with its formidable competitor. He returned to New York to superintend its management in person, but was soon after seized with a sickness, which terminated his life on the 20th January, 1840.—*Playgoers' Journal.*

94. However adroitly the object of these two lines may appear to be concealed, their application can not be mistaken. We freely subscribe to the merits of Mrs. Barnes without feeling in any manner disposed to admit that these merits deteriorate from Mrs. Bartley's. They are distinct in character and effort, and have no relative connection.—*Ed. Nat. Advocate.*

94. SIMON THOMAS, the Caterer-General, indispensible on all such occasions.

96. Mrs. POPPLETON, a Confectioner at 206 Broadway.

97. CHRISTIE kept the principal china and glass store in this city, in Maiden lane.

98. Alluding to a certain individual, whom it was all the fashion to have at all great parties.—*Ed. Eve. Post.*

99. WM. COBBETT, the well known political and infidel writer, having fled to England after the destruction of his press at Philadelphia by a mob about 1795, returned in 1818, settled at New York and opened a seed shop, where he sold ruta baga at a dollar per pound, and black pigs for ten dollars each. For a long space of time, you could hear nothing in Wall or Exchange streets but Cobbett and his black pigs — Cobbett and his ruta baga. * * * Before twelve months he closed the concern, and again sailed for England. Naked he came into America, and naked he returned from thence; his whole goods and chattels (a few minor articles excepted), consisting only of ruta baga and smoked hams from the hind quarters of his black pigs; he shipped one case, however, which by some estimation was beyond all price, viz: a rough Albany deal board, formed into a square box, and in this box was deposited the profound skull and dry bones of the venerated Thomas Paine, author of *Common Sense,* &c. Out of these

bones Cobbett meant to have made political capital, but they were seized by the custom house at London for duty, and sank (if report speaks true) in the deep green sea.—*Grant Thorburn.*

A correspondent in Philadelphia has furnished us several interesting facts relative to Cobbett, during and subsequent to his residence in that city. His establishment there was on North Second street between Market and Arch streets. A difficulty with Governor McKean occasioned a suit, against the result of which he bitterly complained, and while living on Long Island, endeavored to obtain some legislative action at Harrisburgh in his behalf.

In a letter dated Hyde Park (Long Island), September 1st, 1817, after a good deal on farming matters, buckwheat, carrots, cabbages, &c., &c., " all the finest that can be imagined — some of my turnips already weigh about five pounds," and after referring to the treatment received from the government in England, he goes on to say: " In November, I shall go on to Philadelphia, and then I shall tackle the gentry there on account of the proceedings of *McKean*, his *judges* and his *juries*. I am sorry that he and Dallas are dead; for by ——, I will have *justice*; I will have the judgment reversed by act of the assembly, or the whole world shall hear of their injustice and tyranny — they will be cursedly puzzled with me." In a letter dated Harrisbugh, February 10th, 1818, he says: " A report has been made and printed; it is as favorable as it possibly can be; it will come on in the Senate on Saturday."

He was at this time in company with Matthew Carey, between whom and himself there had been much bitterness in 1798, when Carey wrote the *Plumb Pudding for Peter Porcupine*. Our correspondent adds: " While Cobbett was at Long Island in 1817, 1818, 1819, he was experimenting in almost all branches of farming and cattle raising. He was also writing and publishing a grammar and other books, and supplying matter for his *Register*, which was continued in London. He raised various seeds, which were sent to agents in various parts of the United States, put up in packages *sealed*. He induced Mr. Morgan, an admiring friend, to be the agent for Philadelphia. He advertised extensively. I remember a communication in one of the Philadelphia newspapers, the writer of which refers to a letter of Cobbett's to Sir Francis Burdett, in relation to the money which Burdett had lent to him, and asks, who after reading that letter would have so much confidence in Cobbett's honor or honesty as to pay him five dollars for a *sealed* package of seeds or any thing else. It is probable that the allusion in the poem is to this letter. My father-in-law, Mr. William Young, was an extensive bookseller while Cobbett was in Philadelphia. It appears

Cobbett was in his debt, and had to be urged for payment; I find among Mr. Young's papers a note from Cobbett, of which this is a copy:

> 'Good master Young
> I can not send the whole amount,
>   With christian patience watch and wait,
> Take fifty dollars on account,
>   And give the bearer a receipt.
>   Wm. Cobbett.

'P. S.—Though I know it is very difficult to rhyme a Presbyterian out of his money, yet when in the measure of Watts's Psalms and Hymns, it ought to have some weight. I will discharge the rest of your bill as soon as possible, which I hope will be before Saturday night.

'Tuesday, February 5th, 1798.'

"I observe in the extract which you kindly sent to me references to Thorburn, Lockhart's cane, &c., the occasion for which I am unacquainted with; probably the seed business brought him in collision with the eccentric Thorburn, who, it is likely, returned him *quid pro quo.*"

100. GEORGE BARRINGTON was the well known, or rather widely known, light-fingered gentleman to whom is ascribed the witty couplet:

> "True patriots we! For be it understood,
> We left our country for our country's good."—*Allibone.*

101. In a letter from William Cobbett to Sir Francis Burdett, 20th June, 1817, enclosing one to Mr. Tripper, North Hempstead, Long Island, same date, he says: "I beg you to have the goodness to read, and to consider the contents of it (as far as they relate to the liquidation of my debts generally), as addressed to yourself.

"If there be any man who can pretend for one moment, that mine is an *ordinary case,* and, that not having enough to pay every body, I ought to be regarded as an *insolvent debtor,* in the usual acceptance of the words; if there be any man, who wholly absorbed in his attachment to his own immediate interests, is ready to cast blame on a debtor, who has had his means of paying cut off by an operation as decisive as that of an earthquake, which should sink into eternal nothing, his lands, his houses and his goods — if there be any man who, if he had been a creditor of Job, would have insisted that that celebrated object of a malignant devil's wrath, which had swept away his herds, his flocks, his sons and daughters, was an insolvent debtor and a bankrupt, and ought to have been considered such, and as such provided against; if there be any such a man as this to whom I owe any thing, to such a man, I first say that I despise him from the bottom of my soul; and then I say, that if he dare meet me before this world in open and written charge, I pledge myself to cover him with as much shame and infamy as the world can be brought to shower upon so contemptible a being.

———" When the society is too weak or unwilling to defend the property, whether mental or of a more ordinary and vulgar species, and where there is not the will or the power in the society to yield him protection, he becomes clearly absolved of all his engagements of every sort to that society, because in every bargain of every kind, it is understood that both parties are to continue to enjoy the protection of the laws of property."

Sir Francis Burdett replied on the 13th Jan. 1818.

———" It is not my intention to enter into any controversy respecting the honesty or dishonesty of paying or not paying debts according to the convenience of the party owing. It seems that if it should ever suit your convenience and take nothing from the comforts or enjoyments of your family (all this being previously secured), then you think yourself bound to pay your debts; if, on the contrary, that can not be effected without sacrifice on your part, in that case your creditors have no claim. These principles, which are laughable in theory, are detestable in practice. How true is our common law maxim, that no man is an upright judge in his own cause; how truly and prettily said by the French, *La nature se pipe*; no less truly, though more grossly in English, *Nature's her own bawd.*"—*Eve. Post*, 27 *April*, 1819.

102. CoBBETT's seed store was at 63 Fulton street.

103. The poem, *The American Flag*, was published in the *Evening Post*, with the following caption by Mr. Coleman : "Sir Philip Sidney said, as Addison tells us, that he never could read the old ballad of *Chevy Chase*, without feeling his heart beat within him, as at the sound of a trumpet. The following lines, which are to be ranked among the highest inspirations of the Muse, will suggest similar associations in the breast of the gallant American officer."

104. The last four lines of the *American Flag* are by Halleck, in place of the following by Drake, which originally closed the poem :

And fixed as yonder orb divine,
  That saw thy bannered blaze unfurled,
Shall thy proud stars resplendent shine,
  The guard and glory of the world.

105. The meetings of the Forums were held at the City Hotel, in Broadway, on Friday evenings. The price of admission was two shillings.

106. The prominent members of the Forums were J. P. C. Sampson, Orville L. Holley, Thomas G. Fessenden, Hiram Ketchum, &c. The Secretary of the old Forum was Rev. Richard Varick Dey, at one time Chaplain to Congress; and of the New York Forum was Wm. Paxson Hallett, Esq., afterwards Clerk of the United States Court for this district. The valedictory address was delivered by Col. Charles G. Haines.

107. JAMES L. BELL was Sheriff of the County of New York from August 27, 1817, till February 13, 1821.

108. Dawson's Livery Stable, No. 9 Dey street.

109. A. T. GOODRICH's Bookstore, corner of Broadway and Cedar street.

110. EASTBURN's Literary Rooms on the corner of Wall and Nassau streets, where the Custom House now stands.

111. CHESTER JENNINGS came to this city from Connecticut, in search of employment, and engaged as a servant at the City Hotel, then kept by Solomon Gibson. He was soon promoted to the charge of the office of the hotel, and when Mr. Gibson left, in 1816, he became proprietor. Under his management it acquired a high reputation, and Mr. Jennings retired with a competency. His fortune, which was invested in the United States Bank and other stocks, having been swept away by the revulsion of 1837, he was induced by Mr. Astor to resume the management of the hotel, in connection with his former assistant Mr. Willard. Jennings and Willard soon regained their former renown as hotel keepers, and in about five years, Mr. Jennings repaired his losses, and both he and Mr. Willard again retired to private life, Mr. Jennings returning to Connecticut. During a temporary visit to this city, he was taken ill, and died at the Astor House on the 25th

January, 1854, leaving his estate to his sister, Mrs. Otis Munn, of Leyden, N. Y. He was much esteemed for his excellent qualities as a man, and his usefulness as a citizen. The City Hotel, during its existence, was noted, not only for its excellence as a place of entertainment for travellers, but for the accommodations it afforded the citizens for various uses. Dinners to distinguished men, meetings of citizens, concerts, anniversary balls and masonic lodges were held there for many years, while under the auspices of Mr. Jennings, and it will long live in the memories of a large number of the citizens of New York.

112. The death of CATO ALEXANDER was announced in the newspapers of 8th Feb., 1858. For half a century he kept a house of entertainment "on the road," about four miles from the City Hall. Cato's was the fashionable out of town resort for the young men of the day. His suppers were proverbial for excellence, and in sleighing times, it was almost impossible to obtain accommodation for the crowds that frequented the house. His property increased with time. But the fast young men, who had assisted in making Cato rich, occasionally borrowed money of him, at first in small sums and then in larger amounts. In too many instances these were never returned; Cato gradually became crippled in means; his old friends deserted him, while new ones could not be obtained, or were diverted to more attractive places of resort which sprung up in the suburbs of the city. His house was finally sold, and Cato made a last effort to open an oyster saloon in Broadway near Prince street. But he had grown old and infirm, and after a year's trial was obliged to yield; he was no longer seen in that neighborhood, and nothing more was heard of him until his death was announced as above. He died in the 77th year of his age.

113. The Baron VON HOFFMAN, who discharged two pistols in succession at his own body, and missed both times; evidently owing to a want of practice.—*Ed. Eve. Post.*

This Baron Von Hoffman appears to have been all the fashion at this time. He proved to be an arrant imposter, and left this city, but turned up afterwards in Dublin, as the following from the *Evening Post* of 12th June 1823, shows, viz: "Baron Von Hoffman of Sirony, who used to serenade our ladies with the Tyrolese air, so merrily, under their windows in Broadway, a year or two ago, and one day took French leave of them all, now shows away as one of the "nobility and persons of distinction in Dublin."

114. Two lamps are always placed before the door of the house occupied by the Mayor.

115. Allusion is made in this poem, to the names applied to the twenty-eight townships in the Military Tract of Central and Western New York. The soubriquet of "Godfather of the christened west," was now first applied to General De Witt, and he has since been spoken of as entitled to that honor, which, such as it is, is believed to belong to Robert Harper, then Deputy Secretary of State. It appears that the Surveyor General had no share in naming the townships, for in a communication from him to one of the New York papers, he says: "The editor has done the Surveyor General too much honor by retaining for him the naming of the townships in the Military Tract, for a *display of his knowledge*. The names were given by formal resolution of the Commissioners of the Land Office. The Board, consisting of the Governor, the Secretary of State, the Treasurer, the Auditor and the Attorney General, held its meetings in the city of New York. The Surveyor-General had his office established by law in the city of Albany, and *knew nothing of these obnoxious names till they were officially communicated to him*, nor had he even then, any agency in *suggesting* them." General De Witt died in 1834.—*Hist. Magazine*, Vol. iii, No. 3.

As illustrative of the text, we here subjoin a list of the townships whose names were attributed to the Surveyor-General, but as we have seen without justice. They were, Lysander, Hannibal, Cato, Brutus, Camillus, Cicero, Manlius, Aurelius, Marcellus, Pompey, Romulus, Scipio, Sempronius, Tully, Fabius, Ovid, Milton, Locke, Homer, Solon, Hector, Ulysses, Dryden, Virgil, Cincinnatus, Junius, Galen and Sterling. The Legislature of New York in 1835, applied the final touch, suggested in the last stanza, by naming a new town in Onondaga county, De Witt.

116. An expression of Mr. Speaker GERMAN, in allusion to the assessment of property on the borders of the canal.—*Eve. Post*.

117. CATO, the Censor, passed severe sumptuary laws, restraining the extravagant dress of the Roman dandies, and limiting the amount of property which one man might possess, to the sore annoyance of the bankers (or usurers) of Rome. He was also an encourager of home manufactures.—*Eve. Post*.

118. JOHN JOSEPH HOLLAND, arrived in this country in 1796, having been engaged in England by Wignell, as a scene painter for the Philadelphia Theatre. He was afterwards employed to remodel the Park Theatre by Mr. Cooper, who had become the lessee. He was a man of taste in the arts, and his landscapes in water colors had great truth and force.—*Dunlap's Arts of Design.*

119. AMBROSE SPENCER, a native of Salisbury, Connecticut, was admitted to the Bar in 1788. He served in both branches of the State Legislature, and in 1802 was appointed Attorney General of the State. In 1819, he was appointed Chief Justice of the Supreme Court, which office he held until 1823, when he resumed the practice of his profession, but left it after a few years, and retired to private life. He died 13th March, 1848, in the eighty-third year of his age. Mr. Spencer was vehement in speech, and energetic in manner, but kind and approachable to all.—*Street's Council of Revision.*

120. Richard the Third.—*Eve. Post.*

121. JOHN WOODWORTH had then recently been appointed one of the Puisne Justices of the Supreme Court.

122. JAMES TALLMADGE. "Veracity of history compels me to state that in no part of New York, were political bargains more common than among some of the politicians of Dutchess county, and that Mr. Livingston (Peter R.), and Mr. Tallmadge (James) were prominent party leaders in that county."—*Hammond.*

123. Messrs. STEPHEN BATES, GEORGE ROSENCRANTZ and WILLIAM ROSS. The fourth member of the Council of Appointment in that year (1819) was STEPHEN BARNUM, but he appears not to have been acting at this time.

124. A tax of one dollar was imposed by a law of 1817, upon every passenger who traveled over one hundred miles by steam boat upon the Hudson, and of half this sum for every passage over thirty and under one hundred miles. This revenue, with that derived from state lotteries and other sources, was applicable to the construction of canals, and in seventeen years amounted to $73,509.99. The tax was suspended in 1820, and finally ended in 1823.

125. Roger Skinner, a Senator from Sandy Hill, Washington Co., in the eastern district, was a man pleasing in his address; his talents were rather of the persuasive than the solid kind, and, as a companion, he was quite agreeable. He was fond of political management, and rather reckless as to the means he employed to accomplish his ends. He was said to be bitter in his feelings as a partizan. He was, undoubtedly, very much so against Gov Clinton.—*Hammond.*

126. Peter R. Livingston, from Dutchess county, was a man of fine fancy and great declamatory powers. Few men could address a popular assembly with more effect than he. His usefulness as a legislator was impaired by a lack of industry and laborious attention to the details of business. He filled many prominent stations under the state and national governments, and had been a Member of Congress, of the State Senate, and of the Assembly. He died at Rhinebeck on the 19th January, 1847, aged 81 years.—*Hammond & Am. Almanac.*

127. Walter Bowne was this year (1819) elected a member of the State Senate from the city of New York.

128. Messrs. Christian and Warner were Justices of the Peace in this city.

129. George Buckmaster, a perfect Falstaff in proportion, was Alderman of the seventh ward.

130. Pierre C. Van Wyck, an eminent Lawyer and long Recorder of this city. He was a fierce Clintonian, always writing squibs, and contributed with Clinton to the *New York Columbian,* the papers signed A Martling Man. The *Columbian* was edited by Charles Holt.

131. Obadiah German of Chenango county, Speaker of Assembly.

132. Hugh Maxwell, formerly District Attorney of New York, and Collector of the Port—at present residing in Rockland county.

Barent Gardenier, was born in the village of Kinderhook, N. Y., and was the oldest son of Richard Gardenier, a distinguished lawyer of that place. After being admitted to the bar, Barent moved to Ulster county, where he soon rose to eminence. He was elected to represent that county in the 10th Congress. In this new sphere of action, he at once took a distinguished rank and was one of the Federal leaders of the house. In the year 1808, in consequence of severe language used by him in debate, he was assailed with a torrent of personal abuse which provoked a challenge from him and a duel, in which he was shot through the body by George W. Campbell, a member from Tennessee, and barely escaped with his life. At the expiration of his congressional term he moved to the city of New York, where he practiced law for a few years. He afterwards edited the *Examiner*, a periodical published in this city, by his cousin, the late Abraham Vosburgh, Esq. Mr. Gardenier possessed genius of the highest order. He was remarkable for his fascinating address, his soul-stirring eloquence, his brilliant wit and his caustic sarcasm. In the two latter qualities he was but little if any wise inferior to the celebrated John Randolph, by whom he was pronounced the greatest man that ever stood upon the floor of Congress. Mr. Gardenier was a ready and powerful debater, and a bold, frank and fearless man. He died in the city of New York about thirty years ago.

133. GARRET GILBERT, Register of the city and county of New York.

134. PETER H. WENDOVER, was a native of this city and was elected to the State Assembly in 1804, and to the United States Congress in 1815, in which body he served three terms. During the whole time of Mr. Wendover in Congress, he made but one speech, which was upon the altering of the American flag. The flag consisted originally of thirteen stripes and thirteen stars, to which, on the addition of a state to the Union, another stripe, and another star were added. Mr. Wendover urged the appointment of a committee " to inquire into the expediency of altering the flag of the United States." The committee was appointed and reported on the 2d January, 1817, but the " act to establish the Flag of the United States," did not pass until the following year. It was as follows : " Be it enacted, &c., That from and after the fourth day of July next, the flag of the United States be thirteen horizontal stripes, alternate red and white ; that the Union be twenty stars, white in a blue field.

" Sec. 2. And be it further enacted, that on the admission of every new State into the Union, one star shall be added to the Union of the flag ; and that each addition shall take effect on the fourth day of July then next succeeding such admission. Approved April 4, 1818."

Mr. Wendover was afterwards Sheriff of this city.

135. Doctor LAST's examination.—*Eve. Post.*

136. In the stanzas that follow, the literary reader of taste will recognize the plaintive tenderness of the author of Lalla Rookh.— *Ed. Eve. Post.*

137. The Council of Appointment was created in the following manner: "The State for the purpose of electing Senators, was divided into four great districts, the southern, middle, eastern and western. Out of each district, once in every year, the Assembly were required openly to nominate and appoint one Senator, which Senators when thus elected, were, together with the Governor, to form a Council of Appointment. Originally the Governor had the sole power of originating nominations, but in 1801, the constitution was amended so as to give concurrent power of nomination to each member of the Council. The Governor was constituted President of this Board "with the advice and consent of the Council, to appoint all officers" whose appointments were not otherwise provided for in the constitution. All civil and military officers, from the heads of departments, Chancellors and Judges of the Supreme Court, down to, and including all Justices of the Peace and Auctioneers, with the exception of the State Treasurer and a few petty city and town officers, were thus, in effect, appointed by the Governor.—*Hammond.*

The Council of Appointment had become notoriously a political machine, and upon the revision of the constitution in 1821 it was abolished without a dissenting vote, either in the committee or the convention. At the time the Council was discontinued, 8,287 military and 6,663 civil officers held their commissions under this authority, and most of them were liable to removal at will. At an early day, the Council, while it disclaimed the exercise of a judicial authority, felt bound to entertain charges against persons holding office under them, in the presence of the accused, with the view of proving the truth or error of the accusations; but at a later day their proceedings were summary.—*Hough's New York Civil List.*

138. A fashionable tailor in Wall street.

139. Mr. BATES was a shrewd, sensible Yankee. As a county politician, he possessed efficiency, but he was narrow and selfish in his views and principles of action. He was much governed politically, by the impulses of feeling, and of personal likings and dislikings.— *Hammond.*

140. Mr. ROSENCRANTZ was a respectable and worthy Senator, of German descent, from Herkimer county, who, with true Dutch obstinacy, declared he would " never vote for a Bucktail."—*Hammond.*

141. Mr. WILLIAM ROSS, a democratic member from Orange county, though honest and kind-hearted, was a vain man. He was warmly attached to the republican party, but his vanity and want of real talent, rendered him rather a cause of amusement than a terror to his opponents.—*Hammond.*

142. In the proceedings of the Council of Appointment of 10th July 1819, appear the following, viz: " Thomas J. Oakley was appointed Attorney General of the State of New York, in place of Mr. M. Van Buren, removed." " Edward McGaraghan was appointed Justice of the second ward in place of Tennis Wortman, removed." " Jeremiah Drake was appointed Judge of the Marine Court in place of John B. Scott, removed."

143. This piece now appears in Halleck's *Poetical Works*, with the title, *Domestic Happiness*. For the newspaper motto the following is substituted:

" The only bliss
Of Paradise that has survived the fall."—*Cowper.*

144. VANDERVOORT & FLANDIN kept a fashionable dry goods store in Broadway near Park Place.

145. Altered to *More* by the author in *Poetical Works.*

146. The freedom of the Theatre to a resident, or a gold medal of the value of fifty dollars to a non-resident, was offered by the management for the best poetical address to be spoken on the opening night. About sixty communications were received, but the committee awarded the prize to Mr. Charles Sprague of Boston. The address was spoken by Mr. Simpson on the 1st September, 1821. On Monday the 3d, the second prize address by Samuel Woodworth was spoken by Mrs. Barnes, and received much applause.—*Playgoers' Journal.*

147. Mr. OLLIFF was for many years Prompter of the Park Theatre, and had risen from the ranks as a call-boy. He was a remarkably small person, having apparently grown but little since a boy; and his

diminutive person was the cause of infinite merriment. He had as great ambition to be an actor, as to wield the prompter's whistle; and always preferred the part of assassins or robbers, in woods, rocks or ravines, which, contrasted with his small proportions and fierce looks, kept the audience in good humor whenever he assumed a part, which was frequently, as he went on to deliver a message, or fill any occasional vacancy. We believe he is dead, not having heard his whistle in any theatre.—*The Prompter.*

148. The Park Theatre was destroyed by fire July 4, 1821, on the night when Major Noah's play of the *Siege of Tripoli* was performed for the author's benefit. The house was densely filled, and as there was great firing of guns, cannons and small arms in the piece, a company of Marines was present from the navy yard, and it was supposed that the fire originated from the wadding of guns; but this was not the case. It seems that the carpenter's gallery, for convenience, was situated as near to the roof as it could well be, and one of the assistants wanting a tool during the performance, took a light and ascending to the gallery, procured the instrument and left the candle burning on the bench, which after the play had concluded and the audience retired, communicated to the shavings, and in a few minutes the whole house was in flames, and in an hour nothing but the bare walls were left. All the musicians lost their instruments, the actors their wardrobe, and the author the large receipts of the night.—*Prompter.*

149. Messrs. BEEKMAN and ASTOR were joint owners of the theatre for many years; Price and Simpson having paid them more money for rent during their lease than the Theatre had originally cost them, thrice over, they having purchased the building for 50,000 dollars, and leased it for 18,000 dollars per annum.—*Prompter.*

150. JENNINGS for a long time was a celebrated Coat Scourer, well known to the public.

151. SAUNDERS for many years was a celebrated Perruquier in this city, and a man of taste in pictures. He was quite successful in business, having invented a valuable razor strop. Newspaper advertising, in poetry and prose, helped him very much in his business.—*Prompter.*

152. HENRY MEIGS was then a Member of Congress from this city. He was born in New Haven in 1782, graduated at Yale College in 1798, and was elected to Congress from New York city in 1819. He has for many years been Recording Secretary of the American Institute in New York. It is said of him as something remarkable, that he never wore an overcoat, never had a sore throat, or headache, and though nearly eighty years of age does not use glasses. He is a very amiable and worthy gentleman, of great simplicity of character.—*Lanman's Dic. of Congress.*

153. We do not know whether the above address was among the number presented to the literary committee for the premium, at the opening of the Theatre, and rejected; but one thing we will venture to say, there was none offered half so well calculated to produce dramatic effect. And we should hope the managers will present the author with the freedom of the Theatre, by way of encouraging him to make a second effort.—*Ed. Eve. Post.*

154. The poem *To Walter Bowne* was published in the *New York Mirror* with the following preface:

"It gives us great pleasure to be able to lay before our readers an ORIGINAL CROAKER, from the pen of Mr. Halleck. They will find it rich in the same genial humor which is the distinguishing characteristic of the others, and there is throughout a sweeping power of language, and, in the latter part, a sweetness of imagery, that will recommend it to general admiration. It was written for a paper since discontinued, the editor of which has placed us under great obligation, by presenting us with the manuscript."

155. The members of the Council of Appointment for the year 1821, were Walter Bowne from the southern district, John T. Moore from the middle, Roger Skinner from the eastern, and David E. Evans from the western. They were all decidedly hostile, politically, to Governor Clinton, and Mr. Skinner was said to be personally unfriendly to him. From the activity of Judge Skinner, in all party operations, he was supposed to be the most active member of the Council, and it acquired the name of Skinner's Council. He had been educated in a school of politics, which taught him to believe that every legal measure ought to be taken to diminish the power of an opponent, and that to the "victors belong the spoils." This doctrine was carried out with great rigor, much more so than we had ever before been accustomed to.—*Hammond.*

Walter Bowne was descended from an old Quaker family which had been settled at Flushing for many years. He engaged successfully in business in this city, and on his retirement became a prominent politician of the Democratic party. He represented this city in the State Senate for three successive terms, and in 1821 was one of the Council of Appointment. He was afterwards Mayor of the City, which office he held for four years. He was noted in public and private for scrupulous and exact dealings, descending to the smallest details; and by his successful operations, acquired a large estate. He died in this city in August 1846, in the seventy-sixth year of his age.—*Corporation Manual.*

156. CHARLES G. HAINES, a native of New Hampshire, came to New York in the year 1815. He was a man of fine appearance and good address. He wrote much on political subjects, and with great facility and fluency. Mr. Haines was appointed Private Secretary to Governor Clinton, and in 1825 was made Adjutant General of the State, which office he held until his death on the 3d July, 1826.—*Hammond.*

157. The following is from the proceedings of the Council of Appointment of 12th Feb., 1821:

Josiah Hedden, James Hopson and Henry Abel, were appointed Police Justices in place of James Warner, Charles Christian and Charles K. Gardner; Hugh Maxwell, District Attorney in place of Pierre C. Van Wyck; Elisha Morrell, District Justice in place of Thomas Fessenden; M. M. Noah, Sheriff in place of James L. Bell; Everardus Warner, Commissioner of Excise in place of Edward Mc Laughlin; Doctor Jacobus Dyckman, Health Commissioner in place of Peter I. Townsend; Doct. Nicholas Quackenboss, Resident Physician in place of Doctor David Hosack; Abraham Dally, Inspector of distilled spirits in place of Adam Mott; John Brown, Inspector of flour in place of —— Duffy.

158. Mr. Bryant prefaced the poem *To the Recorder,* with the following: "There is a wonderful freshness and youthfulness of imagination in the following epistle, for a septuagenarian if not an octogenarian poet, as the writer must be, if we are to judge from the chronology of his initial lines. He has lost nothing of the grace and playfulness which might have belonged to his best years. The sportive irony of the piece will amuse our readers and offend nobody. Indeed, we are not sure but a part of this is directed against ourselves, but as Mr. Castaly has chosen to cover it up in dashes, it might imply

too great a jealousy of our dignity to make the application, and to mutilate the poem by omitting any part, is contrary to the strict charge of the writer, who insists upon our publishing the whole or none."

159. The Honorable RICHARD RIKER, late Recorder of this city, died on the 26th September 1842, aged 69 years. He held this important office for nearly thirty years, and was esteemed one of the ablest jurisconsults in criminal law, that presided in the courts. He was a gentleman of the old school, always patient, forbearing and attentive, when on the bench, and though an active politician, he made no enemies in private life.—*Am. Almanac.*

160. The duel between Mr. Riker and Mr. Swartwout originated in political quarrel — Mr. R., being an ardent adherent of De Witt Clinton, and Mr. Swartwout a strong personal and political friend of Col. Burr. The duel took place at Wehawken, and Mr. Riker was slightly wounded.

161. As Recorder of the city, he occupied a seat in the Common Council, with the Mayor, who was presiding officer, and always took an active part in the proceedings. He also, with two Aldermen, occupied the bench of the Court of Sessions.

162. A favorite French air. In English "where can one be more happy than in the bosom of one's family."

163. NATHANIEL PITCHER was elected Lieutenant Governor on the same ticket with De Witt Clinton in 1826. He was a warm partizan, and had been an ardent opponent of Gov. Clinton, but the intercourse which he had with the Governor as State Road Commissioner had greatly mollified his feelings towards him. Though zealous as a partizan, Mr. Pitcher was strictly an honest man. By the sudden death of Mr. Clinton, he became Governor of the State. In 1828, Mr. Van Buren was nominated for Governor, and as it was well known that he was to be Secretary of State to General Jackson, and would consequently hold the office but a short time, Mr. Pitcher was greatly mortified at not having received the nomination of Lieutenant Governor, and it made so deep an impression on his feelings, that he never forgave the party who was guilty of it. From that moment, and until the day of his death, he opposed them. He died at his residence in Sandy Hill, Washington county, in 1836. He was four years in the Assembly and three terms in Congress.—*Hammond.*

164. The Commissioners of the Alms House met at stated intervals at Bellevue for the purpose of transacting the business of the department, which, report said, invariably ended with a banquet.

165. The *Pewter Mug*, in Frankfort street, adjoining Tammany Hall, was then, and for many years afterwards, a famous resort for the Democrats.

166. PHILIP HONE was a native of New York, and had resided there, except during a temporary absence in Europe, all his life. He was an Alderman for a long time, and in 1825-26 the Mayor of the city. But his most useful services to the community were rendered as a member of various benevolent and literary institutions. He was one of the earliest and firmest friends of the Mercantile Library Association, and his bust, in marble, done at the request of the Society, adorns the large room of the library. Having been retired from business for a long time, and with an ample fortune, it was in his power to devote his leisure time to the furtherance of objects of general interest and concern. When General Taylor came into the office of President, he was appointed Naval Officer of New York, and was in the discharge of the duties of that office at the time of his death, which took place May 4th, 1851.—*Am. Almanac.*

167. STEPHEN ALLEN's first appearance in political life was in 1817, when he was elected Assistant Alderman of the tenth ward. The public spirit which he manifested induced his friends to bring him forward for the office of Mayor, to which he was appointed by the Common Council for the years 1821 and 1822. He was afterwards elected State Senator, and held the office for several years, and at one time filled the position of Sub-Treasurer of the United States in this city. He was concerned in several banking and insurance companies and in various charitable enterprises; his character for probity and intelligence being a sufficient guaranty for his faithful performance of the most responsible trusts. In his eightieth year, in the summer of 1852, he died, one of the victims of the steam boat Henry Clay, which was burned on the Hudson river near Yonkers.—*Corporation Manual.*

168. JOHN TARGEE was born in Gold street in this city. His father, a Whig of the revolution, left New York during the war, with his family. Mr. Targee was a prominent member of the Tammany Society, and exercised great influence in its proceedings. He held

several important offices in the city, and was a Commissioner of the Alms House for many years.

169. Several inquiries having been made of us respecting the name of the author of an *Epistle to Mr. Hogbin*, published a day or two since in our paper, we took measures to acquaint him with the fact, in order that, if there was no objection on his part, we might satisfy the curiosity of those who had applied to us. This morning we received from him the following note in reply: "The author of the *Epistle to Mr. Hogbin*, has unfortunately no name. His father and mother, in that season of life in which children are generally named, took advantage of his youth and inexperience and declined giving him any. He is therefore compelled to imitate the Minstrel of Yarrow in Leyden's *Scenes of Infancy*, and like him,

   Saves others' names, but leaves his own unsung."
            Eve. Post, Nor. 18, 1830.

170. REYNOLDS kept a Beer House on the corner of Thames and Lumber streets, below the old City Hotel: it was a place of great resort for the Englishmen in the city.

171. JOHN R. LIVINGSTON, at one time a Member of the Assembly from this city.

172. THOMAS APTHORPE COOPER was born in 1776. His father, an Irish gentleman, died in the service of the East India Company, leaving his son to the guardianship of William Godwin, the author of *Caleb Williams*, etc., under whose supervision he received a superior classical education. His attention was early turned to the stage, and at the age of seventeen, he made his first appearance in Edinburg, as Malcolm in Macbeth, but failed completely. Not disheartened, however, he renewed his studies, and at nineteen had appeared at Covent Garden Theatre, as Hamlet and Macbeth, with triumphant success. His first appearance in America, was at Philadelphia, Dec. 9th, 1796, and in August, 1797, played at a Theatre in Greenwich street in this city for the first time. In 1806, he became manager of the Park Theatre, and afterwards associated with him Stephen Price, with whom he continued several years, until he resigned management for the more profitable career of travel. For more than thirty years Mr. Cooper was the paramount favorite of the public, even Cooke's visit leaving his professional reputation entirely unaffected; but the subsequent

appearance of Kean and Macready threw him into comparative neglect, and into a line of characters in which he was ultimately superseded by younger and fresher actors. He accumulated a large fortune by his profession, but his extravagant living finally reduced him to comparative poverty. He made his last appearance in New York at the Bowery Theatre as Duke Aranza, Sept 26th, 1836, but afterwards played at the south. His daughter married a son of President Tyler, who gave him an appointment in the Custom House in this city, which he held for several years. He died at his residence at Bristol, Pa., April 21st, 1849, aged 73 years.—*Playgoers' Journal.*

173. MR. KEAN'S first visit to America was in 1820, and he was very ably supported at the Park Theatre; his engagement being also very profitable to himself. While at Boston, he incurred the displeasure of the audience by refusing to appear, in consequence of a thin house, and was obliged to leave for New York, and shortly afterwards, he returned to England. He made a second visit in 1825; his first appearance being on the 14th November, and the recollection of his slight to the Boston public caused one of the worst riots ever known in the Theatre. He immediately published an apologetic letter, which after a time soothed the public mind, and no farther opposition was made to his performance. In Boston, however, he was not allowed to appear, the recollection of his affront to the audience being too strong to be forgiven. He appeared with some slight opposition, in several other principal cities, and made his last appearance in America, at the Park Theatre as Richard III, December 5th, 1826. He returned to England, but his attraction had greatly diminished, and his dissipated habits served still farther to decrease it. His last appearance was at Covent Garden Theatre in 1833, when he played Othello, to the Iago of his son Charles, but on repeating the sentence "Othello's occupation's gone," he sunk exhausted, and died on the 15th May, 1833, in his 46th year.—*Playgoers' Journal.*

174. Rev. JOHN HENRY HOBART was born in Philadelphia, Sept. 14th, 1775; educated at Princeton, where he graduated in 1793; and in 1798 was ordained deacon by Bishop White, and soon after received the appointment of assistant minister of Trinity Church. In 1811, he was elected Bishop of this diocese, and on the 29th May of that year, was consecrated in Trinity Church, by Bishops White, Provoost and Jarvis. His episcopate lasted twenty-nine years. At the age of fifty-four, while on his progress through the diocese, he suddenly sickened at Auburn, and died there on the 12th Sept., 1830.

175. Mr. JAMES BUCHANAN, for many years British Consul at this port. He died at Montreal, 11th Oct. 1851.

176. HENRY CRUGER, was born in New York city in 1739, educated at Kings College, and in 1757, placed in a Counting House in the city of Bristol. He there became a successful and enterprising merchant, and in 1774 was elected to the British Parliament, as the colleague of the celebrated Edmund Burke. At the parliamentary election in 1780, he was again brought forward as a candidate for Bristol, but defeated, and in 1781 he held the office of Mayor of that city. On the peace in 1783, he visited his native country, and while absent from England he was again elected to parliament in 1784. He finally became a permanent resident of New York in 1790, first residing on the corner of William and Stone streets, in view of Hanover square. Upon the first senatorial election after his return, he was chosen to the State Senate, and held four years, although a question of alienage was raised in consequence of his previous European residence and offices. He died at his residence No. 382 Greenwich street, N. Y., April 24th, 1827, in his eighty-eighth year.—*Van Schaack's Biographical Address.*

177. General MORGAN LEWIS graduated at Princeton College in 1773, and commenced the study of the law in the office of John Jay. In 1774 he joined a volunteer company, and served during the war of the revolution. He was appointed Attorney General of the State in 1791, and afterwards one of the judges of the Supreme Court, and in 1801 became Chief Justice of the State. In 1804, he was elected Governor, but was defeated by Daniel D. Tompkins in 1807. He received the appointment of Major General in 1813, and in 1814 was appointed to the command of the forces destined to the defense of New York. In 1835 he was elected President of the New York Historical Society, and in 1838 President of the Cincinnati State Society, which office he held until his death, on the 7th April, 1844, in the 90th year of his age. "He was a gallant soldier, an accomplished statesman, a kind parent, a benevolent man and a good citizen."

179. JONATHAN B. NICHOLSON, was a Lieutenant, and afterwards Captain in the Navy, and served under Decatur in his action with the Endymion off Long Island, and also in the Mediterranean. He lived and died a bachelor, and was always a gallant and devoted admirer of the ladies.

NOTES. 177

180. Alderman PHILIP BRASHER, a Member of the Legislature from this city eight years, and of great repute as an epicure.

181. Doctor JAMES E. DE KAY was educated as a Physician, but devoted himself from his early years to natural history, and in the State survey of New York, the department of zoology was assigned to him. He died at Oyster Bay, L. I., 8th August, 1851.—*Am. Almanac.*

182. Doctor DAVID HOSACK.

183. The College was originally a stable. One who was once a student in the College says he remembers seeing scratched on the walls in pencil,

> Once a stable for horses,
> Now a College for asses.

184. Doctor WM. HAMERSLEY, Professor of Clinical Medicine, whose almost universal remedy for the cure of pulmonary consumption and heart diseases, was *digitalis.* A quarrel ensued between Doctor Hosack and Doctor Hamersley, relative to the practice of the Hospital, which terminated in the withdrawal of Doctors Hosack, MacNeven, Francis, Mott, &c., and the establishment of the Rutgers Medical College in Duane street.

185. Doctor WILLIAM JAMES MACNEVEN died in this city in July, 1842, in his 79th year. He was a distinguished Irish patriot, and the companion of Thomas Addis Emmet.—*Am. Almanac.*

186. Mr. JAMES TALLMADGE was Lieutenant Governor and presiding officer in the Senate in 1825 and 1826.

187. CLARKSON CROLIUS was born in the sixth ward in this city on the same spot on which his grandfather, who was the first stoneware manufacturer in this city, had settled. In 1802, he was elected by the Republican party Assistant Alderman of the sixth ward, and reëlected until 1805, when he was chosen by the same party as a representative in the State Legislature, in which body his course was such as to inspire confidence in his constituents, who continued him as a member until 1825, when, by the unanimous vote of the House, he was elected Speaker. He had for a number of years presided as Grand Sachem of the Tammany Society, and in 1811 laid the corner stone of Tammany Hall. In 1812, he received a commission as Colonel from President

Madison, and continued in duty at his post at the Narrows until the news of peace in 1815 was received. After 1827 Mr. Crolius was not in active public life. He continued to dwell with the tenacious characteristic of a true Knickerbacker, in the house of his youth, until his death in 1843, in his seventy-first year.

188. The title of the Governor of this State was Commander in Chief of the Army and Navy of the State of New York.

189. Mr. POST was Cashier of the Franklin Bank, and was known as *Whispering Post.*

190. Leslie's picture of Doctor Francis, painted in London in February, 1816.

191. Captain CREIGHTON of the British Navy, a brother of the Rev. Doct. Creighton, who now lives at Tarrytown.

192. In the year 1794, the Corporation of this city petitioned the State Legislature for permission "to set on foot a lottery," in order to raise money to build an Alms House. The Legislature granted their request, and from the proceeds of the lottery, the building in the rear of the City Hall, fronting on Chambers street, was erected, in 1796. In this building the paupers lived until 1816, when they were removed to Bellevue, and the building was granted to the following institutions, viz: The Academy of the Fine Arts, the New York Historical Society, the Literary and Philosophical Society, the Lyceum of Natural History, the Deaf and Dumb School, the Board of Health, and Scudder's Museum. All these took possession in 1816, and the building was called the New York Institution. About 1840, these societies had all left the building, and it was occupied by the Marine Court and the Court of Sessions, which in turn gave way to the Law Library and various offices, under the name of the New City Hall. It was burned down in January, 1856.

The American Academy of Arts was established in 1802, and was incorporated in 1808, with Robert R. Livingston as President and Col. John Trumbull, Vice President. Mr. Livingston, while living in Paris, as Ambassador, purchased a number of casts for the use of the Academy and sent them to this city. They were exhibited in Greenwich street, with such paintings and works of art as could be collected for the purpose. The Academy languished, however, until 1816, when De Witt Clinton, then President, assisted by Dr. Hosack, Cadwallader D. Colden, and some other gentlemen, made a strong effort to revive it, and opened an exhibition in October of that year in the building in the Park fronting on Chambers street, which had been recently occupied as an Alms House, but a portion of which had been set apart by the corporation for their use.—*Dunlap's Arts of Design.*

193. In September, 1818, Mr. JAMES W. WALLACK made his first appearance before a New York audience as Macbeth, and met with triumphant success. He was born in London in 1794, and appeared at Drury Lane Theatre in 1812 as Laertes. His reputation soon increased, and in parts of a melo-dramatic cast he was soon without a rival. He was a careful student, and cultivated his powers unceasingly; the results of which are plainly perceptible in every character he attempts. He made several visits to this country, and in 1837 became Manager of the National Theatre in Leonard street, which was burned in 1839, when he returned to Europe. He was again in this country in 1843, and played at the Park Theatre. In 1852, he undertook the management of the present Wallack's Theatre, where by gathering around him an excellent company, and by the superior taste and judgment which he showed in the production of the pieces represented, he gave general satisfaction to the public. Mrs. Bartley was a great favorite with the New York public. She made her first appearance in the character of *Isabella* on the 18th November, 1818. She had previously performed the leading parts in tragedy at Drury Lane Theatre, and after remaining a few years in this country returned to London, and played at Covent Garden Theatre. The melalogue referred to in the poem was written for her by Thomas Moore, and recited by her for the first time on the occasion of her benefit at the Park Theatre on the 10th April, 1819, with appropriate musical accompaniments by the orchestra.—*Playgoer's Journal.*

194. Doctor HORNE, of notorious memory. The motto at the head of his advertisement was, "*Salus Populi Suprema Lex.*"

195. Doctor DE ANGELIS'S *Four-herb Pills*, were advertised as a specific for all human infirmities.

196. ADAM GEIB, Keeper of a Music Store at No. 23 Maiden lane, taught an "analytical" system of music.

INDEX.

Abel, Henry, 171.
Abiram, 5.
Abstract of Surgeon-General's Report, 42.
Academy of Arts, to the Directors of, 124.
Academy of the Fine Arts, 178.
Adams, John Quincy, 86.
Addison, 160.
Address for opening of New Theatre, 84.
Admiral, 119.
Adjutant General, 171.
Adonis, 68.
Agamemnon, 90.
Aladdin's Lamp, 51.
Albany, 38, 99, 119, 154, 157, 163.
Albin, 47.
Alcides, 112.
Alderman, City, 75.
Aleck, 6.
Alexander, Cato, 162.
Allen, Stephen, 102, 130, 173.
Alms House, 173, 174, 178, 179.
Altorf, 2, 138.
Ambition, 119.
American Academy of Arts, 178.
American Flag, 59, 160, 166.
American Institute, 170.
Angelis, 130.
Annapolis, 146.
Aranza, Duke, 175.
Arab, 92.
Arcadian Vale, 102.
Arch street, Philadelphia, 158.
Ariel, 94.
Arts, Academy of, 124.

Ashe, 42.
Astor, John Jacob, 84, 161, 169.
Astor House, 161.
Atlantic, 30.
Atropos, 19.
Attorney General, 163, 164, 168.
Auburn, 175.
Auditor, State, 163.
Aurelius, 163.
Backwood, 26.
Backwoodman, 48.
Bacon, 76, 105.
Bacon, Ezekiel, 11, 143.
Baehr, 79.
Bailey, Benjamin, 40, 102, 155.
Bailey & Bogert, 155.
Bainbridge, Commodore, 152.
Bajazet, 74.
Baldwin, Charles N., 2, 138.
Balls, 66.
Baltimore, 146, 150.
Bank Coffee House, 156.
Bankrupt Law, 50, 138.
Banks, 2, 57, 71.
Banquo's Ghost, 8.
Barclay Street, 37, 116, 129, 154.
Barker, Jacob, 150.
Barnes, John, 35, 153.
Barnes, Mrs., 13, 138, 156, 157, 168.
Barnes, Mrs., Address to, 51.
Barnes, Miss Charlotte, 156.
Barnum, Stephen, 164.
Baron Toraldi, 36.
Barriere, 138.
Barrington, George, 57, 159.
Bartley, Mrs., 128, 157, 179.

INDEX.

Bashaws, 79.
Bates, Stephen, 79, 164, 167.
Battery, 2, 133.
Battery Enlargement, 147
Battery Tax, 33.
Battery War, 16.
Bayard, William, 8, 142.
Bear, 76.
Beatrice, 52.
Beauty's bark, 78.
Beauty and the Beast, 76.
Beekman, 36, 84, 151, 169.
Bell, James L., 65, 89, 161, 171.
Belino, 35, 153.
Belles Lettres Repository, 144.
Bellevue, 99, 125, 133, 173, 178.
Beersheba, 118.
Bertram, Henry, 150.
Beverly, 52.
Bibles, Wood Cuts for, 125.
Big Little Dry, 69.
Black Apollo, 54.
Blackstone, 47.
Blackwell's Isle, 99.
Blackwood, 26.
Bloodgood, Abraham, 5, 140.
Bloomingdale, 99.
Blue Monday, 105.
Board of Health, 78.
Bob Acres, 92.
Bobadil, 76.
Bogardus, Gen. Robert, 5, 8, 17, 37, 39, 133, 141, 147.
Bonaparte, 17, 31.
Bony, 7, 64, 133.
Bones of Thomas Paine, 157.
Borough Mongers, 57.
Boston, 144, 150, 153, 168, 175.
Botley, 57.
Bowery Theatre, 150, 175.
Bowne, Walter, 75, 89, 165, 170, 171.
Bowne, Walter, Address to, 87.
Box presented to Andrew Jackson, 138, 139.
Bracket, Joseph W., 40, 155.
Brasher, Alderman Philip, 107, 108, 177.
Brevet Appointments, 43, 141.
Brighton Theatre, 150.
Bristol, Eng., 176.
Bristol, Pa., 175.
British Plutarch, 69.
Broad Street, 146.

Broadway, 12, 56, 68, 116, 142, 146, 147, 154, 161, 162, 168.
Bronaugh, Dr. 6, 141.
Browere, Praxiteles, 95.
Brown, Gen. Jacob, 152.
Brown, John, 171.
Brummagem, 68.
Brutus, 18, 29, 71, 149, 163.
Bryant, William C., 101, 171.
Buchanan, James, 107, 108, 176.
Buckets, Champion of, 25.
Buckmaster, George, 76, 165.
Bucks, 75.
Bucktails, 5, 34, 66, 123, 140, 152, 168.
Bull, Johnny, 30.
Bulls, 66.
Bunker's Hill, 63.
Burdett, Sir Francis, 159, 160.
Burgundy, 99.
Burke, Edmund, 176.
Burleigh, Lord, 13.
Burnett, Gen. Ward B., 139.
Burr, Aaron, 142, 172.
Byrne, 127.
Byron, Lord, 48.
Cabbage, Paulding's, 48, 149.
Cacafogo, 75.
Caesar, Julius, 91, 92, 93.
Caesars, 133.
Camillus, 163.
Campbell, Tom, 48.
Campbell, George W., 166.
Canals, 2, 66.
Capitol, Washington, 146.
Captain General, 119.
Carey, Matthew, 158.
Cassius, 18.
Castaly, Thomas, 91, 171.
Castlereagh, Lord, 57.
Castor and Pollux, 19.
Cato, 68, 71, 163.
Cato the Censor, 71, 163.
Cedar Street, 161.
Censor, 71.
Cerro Gordo, 139.
Chambers Street, 178, 179.
Chancellor, 167.
Charleston, South Carolina, 139.
Chatham Street, 155.
Chatham Theatre, 145.
Chenango County, 10, 143.
Cherry Street, 56, 154.
Cherubusco, 139.

INDEX. 183

Chevy Chase, 160.
Chief Justice Supreme Court, 164, 176.
Chippewa, 63.
Chloe, 45, 46, 155.
Choctaws, 50.
Christian, Charles, 40, 75, 89, 155, 165, 171.
Christie, 54, 157.
Chronicle, 12.
Cicero, 163.
Cincinnati, State, 176.
Cincinnatus, 163.
City Aldermen, 75.
City Hall, Nashville, Tenn., 139.
City Hall, New York, 37, 65, 139, 143, 152, 161, 162, 174, 178.
City Hotel, 161, 174.
Clark, Lewis and, 69.
Clinton, De Witt, 2, 7, 20, 34, 40, 41, 66, 74, 79, 80, 89, 123, 130, 131, 132, 140, 141, 144, 148, 152, 155, 165, 170, 171, 172, 178.
Clinton's Speech, 118.
Clintonians, 40, 122, 143, 165.
Cobbett, Wm., 57, 58, 157, 158, 159, 160.
Cobbett, Wm., Loving Epistle to, 57.
Coffee House, 29.
Colden, Gen. Cadwallader D., 5, 6, 37, 133, 138, 140, 141, 178.
Coleman, William, 12, 48, 145, 148, 150, 153, 155, 160.
Coleraine, 99.
Columbia College, 141.
Columbian, 138.
Columbian Order, 154, 155.
Commander-in-Chief, 178.
Commissioner of Alms House, 173, 174.
Commissioners of Land Office, 163.
Common Council, 172, 173.
Common Sense, 157.
Congress Halls, 71.
Connecticut, 161.
Connewango Creek, 121.
Constitution, New, 85.
Contreras, 139.
Covent Garden Theatre, 174, 175, 179.
Coodies, 34, 40, 152.
Coody, Abimelech, 152.

Cooke, 76, 146, 174.
Cooper, Thomas Apthorpe, 107, 108, 127, 144, 156, 164, 174.
Coquette, Address to an Elderly, 45.
Cornwallis, Surrender of, 146.
Costar, John G. 147.
Council Chamber, 99.
Council of Appointment, 75, 171.
Council of Appointment, Address to, 79, 137, 144, 164, 167, 168, 170.
Count Belino, 35, 153.
Court of Sessions, 172, 178.
Crabbe, 48.
Creighton, Capt., 126, 178.
Creighton, Rev. D., 178.
Croaker & Co., 18.
Croaker, Junior, Address to, 18.
Crolius, Clarkson, 118, 155, 177, 178.
Cruger, Henry, 108, 176.
Curtain Conversations, 82.
Custom House, 161, 175.
Cythera, 125.
Dallas, 158.
Dally, Abraham, 171.
Dan, 118.
Danæ, 126.
Dandies, 16, 55, 68, 71.
Dash, Mrs., 83.
Dathan, 5.
David's College, 24, 130.
Dawson, 66, 161.
De Angelis, Dr., 179.
Deaf and Dumb School, 178.
Death in Blue Beard, 76.
Decatur, 176.
Declaration of Independence, 146.
D. K. Tea Party, 110, 111.
De Kay, Dr. James E., 177.
Delaplaine, Joseph, 148.
Delaplaine's Repository, 24, 148.
Democratic, 152, 171.
Democratic Gen. Committee, 155.
Desdemona, 52.
Design, 14.
De Stael, Madame, 1.
Detraction, 64.
Devil's Bridge, 153.
De Witt, Simeon, 72, 163.
De Witt, Simeon, Surveyor-General, Address to, 69.
De Witt Township, 72, 163.

184 INDEX.

Dey, Richard Varick, 63, 161.
Dey Street, 161.
Dickens, 16.
Diddler, 76.
Digitalis, 116, 177.
Dinah, 52.
Dinner Party, 107.
District Att'y., New York, 165, 171.
Doctors, King of the, 116.
Doe, John, 98.
Dogberry, 75, 89.
Domestic Happiness, 168.
Domestic Peace, Address to, 33.
Doodle, 75.
Doyle, Dennis H., 5, 141.
Drake, J. R., 139, 160.
Drake, Jeremiah, 80, 168.
Drury Lane Theatre, 156, 179.
Dryden, 163.
Duane Street, 177.
Dublin, 162.
Duels, 166.
Duff, Mr., 153.
Duffy, 89, 171.
Duke Aranza, 175.
Dunlap, 144.
Dutchess County, 164, 165.
Dyckman, Dr. Jacobus, 171.
Dyckman, Lt. Col. Garret, 139.
Eastburn, 66.
Eastburn's Literary Rooms, 161.
East India Company, 174.
Eden, 82.
Eden's Bower, 77.
Edinburgh, 174.
Edinburgh Review, 1.
Edwin, William, 152.
Edwards, 5.
Elijah, 22.
Elisha, 22.
Eleusinian Mysteries, 103.
Eloquence, 64.
Emmet, Thomas Addis, 177.
Endor, Witch of, 125.
Endymion, 127, 176.
England, 9, 25, 58, 146, 152, 157, 158, 164, 175, 176.
Ennui, Address to, 1.
Envy, 64.
Equality, 14.
Erie, 121.
Erie Canal, 140.
Europe, 7, 70, 133, 142, 146, 173, 179.

Eveleen's Bower, 36.
Evening Post, 145, 146, 147, 148, 160, 162.
Evening Star, 137.
Examiner, 166.
Exchange Street, 157.
Fabius, 163.
Faction, 94.
Falstaff, 76, 150, 154, 165.
Fame, 69.
Fancy's Sketch, 36.
Fanny, Poem entitled, 151.
Fashionable Folly, 54.
Faustus, 31.
Feds, 34, 40.
Federalism, 152.
Fessenden, Squire, 89.
Fessenden, Thomas G., 161, 171.
Fine Arts, Academy of, 178.
Firth & Hall, 154.
Fitz, 1.
Flag, American, 59, 160, 166.
Flandin, 83, 168.
Flushing, 95, 171.
Fly Market, 16.
Forest Rose, 145.
Fortune, 66.
Fortune, Ode to, 65.
Forums, The, 62, 64, 128, 161.
Forum Hall, 63.
Forty Thieves, 75.
Four-herb Pills, 179.
France, 138.
Francis, Day, 128.
Francis, Dr., 125, 177, 178.
Francis, Sir, 58.
Frankfort Street, 99, 155, 173.
Franklin Bank, 37, 65, 154, 178.
Franklin's Bust, 32, 152.
Franklin Square, 154.
Franklin, Walter, 154.
Fredon, 148.
Frede, 148.
Freedom, 59, 61, 96, 123.
Freedom, Champion of, 25.
Freedom of the City, 3.
Fredonian, 148, 123.
Free School Trustee, 112.
French, 55.
French Leave, 83, 162.
Fundable, 114, 115.
Fundy, Bay of, 118.
Fulton Street, 58, 160.
Galen, 71, 163.

INDEX.

Gallic Thunderbolt, 125.
Gander, Party's, 94.
Garcia, 103, 153.
Garden Seeds, 58.
Gardner, Charles K., 17, 171.
Gardenier, Barent, 76, 165, 166.
Gardenier, Richard, 165.
Garner, William, 30, 150.
Geib, Adam, 130, 179.
Gemini, 19.
German Doll, 68.
German, Obadiah, 11, 70, 76, 143, 163, 165.
Giant Wife, 76.
Gibson, Solomon, 161.
Gilbert, Garret, 166.
Gingerbread Guards, 17.
Godfather of the Christened West, 70, 163.
Godwin, William, 174.
Gold Box, 3, 139.
Gold Street, 173.
Goodrich, A. T., 66, 161.
Goodrich, 66.
Gore, Christopher, 146.
Governor, 38, 119, 122, 140, 146, 154, 163, 167, 178.
Governor, titles of, 178.
Gracchus, 71.
Graces, 31.
Grammars, Cobbett's, 58.
Grand Council, 154.
Grand March of Mind, 104.
Grand Sachem, 154, 177.
Great Britain, 25, 177.
Grecian, 62.
Greece, 120.
Green River, 101.
Greenwich, 133.
Greenwich Street, 174, 176.
Grocers, meeting of the, 114.
Grog, 43.
Guards, 66.
Guardsmen, 2.
Guido, 14.
Guido's Hours, 95.
Guinea, 55.
Hackett, James, 145.
Haff, Capt., 76.
Haff, John, 40.
Haff, John P., 5, 140, 154.
Haines, Col. Charles G., 89, 120, 161, 171.
Hallam, 144.

Halleck, 102, 151, 160, 168, 170.
Hallett, William Paxson, 63, 161, 170.
Hamblin, Thomas S., 144.
Hamersley, Dr. Wm., 177.
Hamilton, Alexander, 20.
Hampden, 70.
Hampstead Parnassus, 47.
Handy, Sir Abel, 149.
Hannibal, 163.
Hanover Square, 152, 176.
Hanover Street, 152.
Haram's Cages, 64.
Harlem, 99.
Harlequin, 74.
Harmodius, 96.
Harper, Robert, 163.
Harrisburgh, 158.
Hartman, Lewis, 16, 147.
Havana, 148.
Hawkins, 140.
Hawkins, Micah, 2, 5, 138, 140.
Hamlet, 174.
Haytian Grooms, 68.
Hecate, 75.
Hector, 163.
Hedden, Josiah, 171.
Hempstead, 57.
Henry Clay (steamer), 173.
Herkimer County, 168.
Hermes, 120.
Herring, 120.
He Stoops to Conquer, 149.
Hillhouse, 101.
Historical Society, N. Y., 178.
Hobart, Rt. Rev. John Henry, 107, 109, 175.
Hoboken, 9, 137, 142.
Hodgkinson, 144.
Hogbin, Robert, 104, 105, 106, 174.
Hogbin, Robert, Epistle to, 104.
Holland, John Joseph, 73, 164.
Holley, Orville L., 161.
Holt, Charles, 165.
Homer, 70, 163.
Hone, Doctor, 179.
Hone, Philip, 100, 173.
Hope, 38.
Hopper, Mr., 13, 145.
Hopson, James, 171.
Horace, 48.
Horne, 129, 131.
Horne, Doctor, 179.

Hosack, Dr. David, 56, 130, 131, 171, 177, 178.
Howard, James, 30, 150.
Hudson River, 164, 173.
Hudson Steam boats, 164.
Humane Society, 112.
Hunt, 57.
Hunt, Leigh, 47.
Hurtell, 120.
Hyde Park, L. I., 158.
Hydra Modern, 112.
Iago, 175.
Ilissus, 62.
Imogen, 52.
Impudence, Ode to, 49.
Incledon, 153.
Invisible Girl, 29.
Isabella, 179.
Israelite, 151.
Italian Opera, 153.
Italy, 120.
Jackson, Gen. Andrew, 2, 8, 138, 139, 140, 141, 142, 172.
Jacobinism, 152.
Jamaica, 21, 145.
Jarvis, Bishop, 175.
Jarvis, John Wesley, 3, 34, 152.
Jay, John, 176.
Jay Treaty, 146.
Jefferson, 30, 154.
Jennings, Chester, 66, 161, 162.
Jennings (scourer), 85, 169.
Jersey City, 141.
Jessy Oatland, 145.
Jews upon Grand Island, 137.
Jobson, 75.
John Bull, 68.
Johnny Bull, 30.
Johnson, 31, 42.
Johnny, 16.
Joseph Surface, 74.
Julia, 155.
Juliet, 52.
Junius, 71, 163.
Justice Shallow, 74.
Kean, 107, 175.
Keene, 153.
Kemble, 29.
Ketch, Jack, 80.
Ketchum, Hiram, 161.
Killings, 80.
Kilner, 30.
Kilner, Thomas, 149.
Kinderhook, 165.

King, Charles, 8, 16, 141, 147.
King Dick, 74.
King, Mr., 156.
King of the Doctors, 116.
King, Rufus, 20, 21.
King Street, 156.
King's College, 176.
Knickerbacker, 178.
Korah, 5.
Lady Randolph, 156.
Laertes, 179.
Lafayette Theatre, 150.
Laight, 133.
Lalla Rookh, 167.
Lament for Great Ones Departed, 37.
Lang, John, 150, 151.
Lang, John, Address to, 31.
Lang, Johnny, 32.
Langstaff, 111.
Langstaff, Dr., 1, 137.
Last, Dr., 76, 166.
Laurens Street, 150.
Law Library, 178.
Lawrence, Dr. John M., 139.
Leavenworth, 55.
Lebanon, Ct., 146.
Leesugg, Miss Catharine, 13, 145.
Leghorn Hats, 80.
Lempriere, 69.
Lent, James, 17, 148.
Leonard Street, 145, 157, 179.
Leslie, 178.
Lewis County, 142.
Lewis & Clarke, 69.
Lewis, General Morgan, 108, 109, 176.
Leyden, N. Y., 162.
Leyden's Scenes of Infancy, 174.
Lingo, 153.
Lit. and Phil. Society, 178.
Lives of Distinguished Americans, 148.
Livingston, John R., 174.
Livingston, Peter R., 75, 164, 165.
Livingston, Robert R., 178.
Livy, 71.
Locke, 163.
Lockhart's Cane, 57, 159.
London, 48, 80, 156, 158, 178, 179.
London Tailors, 68.
Long Island, 57, 158, 159, 176.
Long Island Star, 138.
Lord Burleigh, 13, 74.

INDEX.

Lord Chamberlain, 117.
Lord Grizzle, 75.
Lottery Shark, 2.
Lottery Alms House, 178.
Love of Notoriety, 67.
Love's Young Dream, 36.
Loving Epistle to Cobbett, 57.
Lumber Street, 174.
Lucifer, 22.
Lyceum of Natural History, 178.
Lynch, Dominick, 34, 53, 153.
Lysander, 163.
McEvers, 142.
Mat, 108.
Macbeth, 29, 110, 174, 179.
McGaraghan, Edward, 80, 168.
McGarraghan, Squire, 17.
Macbeth, Charley's, 29.
McKean, Gov., 158.
McLaughlin, Edward, 89, 171.
MacNeven, Dr. Wm. James, 177.
Macready, 175.
McSycophant, Sir Pertinax, 146.
Madagascar Bat, 2.
Madison, President, 137, 154, 178.
Magenis, 127.
Maiden Lane, 88, 157, 179.
Malbrook, 33.
Malcolm, 174.
Manlius, 163.
Mapes, Gen. Jonas, 40, 133, 155.
Marcellus, 163.
Marine Court, 178.
Market street, Phila., 158.
Marshall, Chief Justice, 2, 50, 138.
Martling, Abraham, 11, 140, 143.
Martling's Long Room, 155.
Martling Man, 165.
Massachusetts, 144, 145.
Mathurin, 52.
Maxwell, Hugh, 76, 165, 171.
Maywood, Robert Campbell, 13, 145, 146.
Mayor, 75, 95, 140, 171.
Mead, 5, 140.
Meadows, Hoboken, 142.
Mecca, 89.
Meddler, 76.
Mediterranean, 176.
Meigs, 28, 40, 76.
Meigs, Henry, 17, 28, 40, 76, 86, 149, 170.
Mercantile Library Association, 193.

Mercein, Thomas R., 17, 147, 148.
Mercer, Mrs., 156.
Merry Dames, 149.
Mexican War, 139.
Midas, 27.
Military Tract, 163.
Militia The, 121, 132.
Militia defined, 42.
Miller, Judge, 88, 120.
Miller, Sylvanus, 11, 144.
Milton, 71, 80, 163.
Minstrel of Yarrow, 174.
Minshull, John, 25, 26, 148, 149.
Mirth, 34.
Mississippi, 140.
Missouri, 86.
Mitchill, Samuel L., 23, 31, 38, 47, 54, 76, 86, 130, 131, 143, 155.
Modern Hydra, 112.
Malbrook, 33.
Momus, 1.
Monroe, 86.
Montreal, 176.
Montgomery, 48.
Montgomery, Master, 108.
Monument upon Grand Island, 137.
Mooney, William, 154.
Moore, John T., 170.
Moore Thomas, 48, 179.
Morgan, Lady, 1, 138, 158.
Morgiana, 51.
Moreland, Harry George, 30, 150.
Morocco, (read Tunis), 137.
Morrell, Elisha, 89, 171.
Morris, General, 145.
Morton, Maj. Gen, 141.
Mott, Adam, 89, 171.
Mott, Doctor, 177.
Mumford, Gurdon S., 5, 120, 141.
Mummy Chogs, 148.
Munn, Mrs. Otis, 162.
Murray, Col., 147.
Murray's Guards, 33.
Nashville, 139.
Nassau Street, 143, 155, 161.
National Advocate, 137.
National Painting, 14.
National Theatre, 145, 157, 179.
Natural Bridge, Va., 30.
Naval Officer, 173.
Nestor, 71.
New Bowery, 154.
New Brighton, 154.

New City Hall. **178.**
Newgate, 57.
New Hampshire, **171.**
New Haven, 144, **170.**
New Jersey, 142.
New Orleans, 155.
Newton, 81.
New York, 138, 139, 141, 142, 143, 144, 145, 146, 148, 149, 150, 151, 152, 153, 154, 157, 161, 162, 163, 164, 165, 166, 170, 171, 173, 175, 176, 177, 178, 179.
New York Columbian, 138, **165.**
New York Enquirer, 187.
New York Gazette, 81, **150, 151,** 152.
New York Hist. Society, **152, 176,** 178.
New York Institution, 178.
New York Mirror, 145, 170.
New York Volunteers, 139.
Niagara River, 137.
Niblo, William, 29, 66, 156.
Niblo's Garden, 150, 156.
Nicholson, John B., 109, 176.
Nightmare, The, 122.
Nipperkin, 75.
Noah, 113.
Noah, Major Mordecai M., **1, 12,** 187, 169, 171.
Noah's Ark, 84.
Noodle, 75.
North Dutch Church, Albany, 154.
North Hempstead, L. I., 57, 159.
North Second street, Phila., 158.
North River, 62.
Notoriety, Love of, 67.
Nova Scotia, 158.
Oakley, Thomas J., **80, 168.**
Oberon, 97.
Ohio, 150.
Old England, 26.
Olympic Theatre, 146.
Oliff, 13, 36, 84, 86, 168.
Oneida County, 143.
Onondaga County, 163.
Orange County, 168.
Orleans, 118.
Ostler, Tom, 16.
Oswego County, 143.
Othello, 175.
Overreach, 74.
Ovid, 163.

Oyster Bay, 177.
Paine, Thomas, 157.
Painting, National, 14.
Pangloss, 74.
Paris, 108, 178.
Park, 2, 4, 8, 89, 48, 106, 133, 179.
Park Place, 168.
Park Theatre, 138, 144, 145, 149, 150, 153, 154, 156, 157, 164, 168, 169, 174, 175, 179.
Parliament, 176.
Parnassus, Hempstead, 47.
Paulding, James K., 25, 26, **28, 48,** 70, 149.
Peace, 33, 84.
Paul Pry, 103.
Pearl Street, 138, 151, **152.**
Pell, Colonel, 133.
Pell, Ferris, 8, 76, 89, **120, 141.**
Pennsylvania Jail, 57.
Peter Porcupine, 58.
Pewter Mug, 99, 173.
Philadelphia, 137, 138, 146, 148, 150, 153, 156, 157, 158, 174, 175.
Philadelphia Theatre, **164.**
Phœbus, Judge, 48.
Phi Beta Kappa, 86.
Phillips, T., 12, 35, 127, **153.**
Phillipse's Mansion, 156.
Phlogobombos, 23.
Phoca's Gullet, 126.
Pierson's Factory, 5.
Pillow, Gen., 139.
Pinckney William, 146.
Pine Street, 156.
Pistol, 76.
Pitcher, Nathaniel, 99, 172.
Plandome, 148.
Pleaid, Lost, 90.
Plum Pudding for Peter Porcupine, 158.
Pluto, 128.
Poetical Address Premium for, 168.
Polony, 126.
Pollissons, 98.
Pompey, 163.
Ponder, 75.
Poppleton, Mrs., 54, 66, 157.
Post, 120.
Post, Mr., 178.
Potter, Mr., 10, 11, 128, 142.
Presbyterian, 159.
Presenting Freedom of the City, 3.

INDEX. 189

Provost, Bp., 175.
Price, Stephen, 51, 74, 144, 156, 157, 174.
Prime, 54, 169.
Prime, N., 18, 148.
Prime, Ward and King, 148.
Prince Regent, 30.
Prince Street, 162.
Princeton, 175, 176.
Pritchard, 138.
Prog, defined, 43.
Promethean Fire, 68.
Protestant Episcopal Theological School, 146.
Puisne Justices Sup. Court, 164.
Pygmalion, 106.
Quackenboss, Dr. Nicholas, 171.
Quackery, Address to, 129.
Quarantine, 154.
Ramsay, Marian, 145.
R——, Johnny, 107, 108.
Randolph, John, 166.
Randolph, Lady, 156.
Reade Street, 147.
Rebellion, 116.
Recorder, 171, 172.
Recorder ——, Poetical Epistle to, 91.
Red Notes, 31.
Regents, 117.
Register, Cobbett's, 58, 158.
Republican Chronicle, 138.
Resignation of General Washington, 146.
Reynolds, 104, 174.
Rhinebeck, 165.
Richard III, 145, 164, 175.
Richmond Hill Theatre, 153.
Riker, Richard, 38, 91, 92, 93, 96, 172.
Robbins, Levi, 10, 128, 142.
Robert, 16, 108.
Robin Adair, 36.
Rockland County, 165.
Roe, Richard, 98.
Rogers, 48.
Roman, 30, 62, 163.
Romans, 92.
Rome, 94, 98, 163.
Romulus, 163.
Root, Erastus, 10, 11, 20, 75, 143.
Rosalind, 52.
Rose, 5.
Rosencrantz, George, 79, 164, 168.

Ross, William, 79, 164, 168.
Rubens, 125.
Rubicon, 93.
Rumor, Miss, 1.
Rural Felicity, 148.
Ruta Baga Turnips, 57, 157.
Rutgers' Med. College, 177.
St. Mark's Burying Ground, 153.
St. Tammany, 102.
Salisbury, Ct., 164.
Salmagundi, 130.
Sampson, J. P. C., 161.
Sancho, 97, 119.
Sandy Hill, Wash. Co., 165, 172.
Saratoga, 146.
Saunders, 85, 169.
Saw Mill, the, or a Yankee Trick, 138.
Scenes of Infancy, 174.
Scipio, 70, 163.
Scoles, 149.
Scotch Mist, 29.
Scott, 47, 80.
Scott, John B., 168.
Scribble, Mr., 16.
Scudder, 125.
Scudder's Museum, 178.
Secret Mine, 5.
Secretary of State, 163.
Seed Store, Cobbett's, 160.
Seminole Compaign, 141.
Sempronius, 163.
Septon, 23.
Shakespeare, 13.
Shaking Quakers, 120.
Sharpe, Peter, 11, 143.
Shelley, 42.
Sherman, Alpheus, 155.
Sherred, Jacob, 15, 107, 108, 146.
Shiell, 52.
Sidney, Sir Philip, 160.
Siege of Tripoli, 169.
Signal Poles, 31.
Simon, 55.
Simon, the Cook, 54.
Simpson, E., 12, 29, 144, 156, 168, 169.
Simpson E., Address to, 35, 73.
Sing Sing, 99.
Sirony, 162.
Skaats, Bartholomew, 3, 139, 140, 143.
Skinner, Roger, 75, 165, 170.
Slander, 64, 94.

Society Ref. Juv. Delinquents, 140.
Solomon, 151.
Solon, 163.
South Carolina, 139.
Southey, 48.
Smith Street, 156.
Speaker of Assembly, 11.
Speech, Mr. Clinton's, 17.
Spencer, Ambrose, 74, 85, 164.
Spirit of Laws, 48.
Spooner, Alden, 2, 129, 138.
Sprague, Charles, 168.
Spruce Street, 143, 155.
Sprightly Widow, &c., 148.
Squaretoes, Old, 55.
Stage of State, 74.
Staten Island, 38, 154.
Staten Island's Summer Seat, 37.
Steddiford, 133.
Steamboat Tax, 75, 144.
Sterling, 163.
Steuben March, 68.
Sturges & Crowninshield, 138.
Stewart, A. T., 142, 147.
Styx, 128.
Sunday Times, 137.
Sub Treasurer of U. S., 173.
Surgeon General, Address to, 23.
Surgeon General, 23, 117, 155.
Surgeon General's Report, 42.
Surgeon's Hall, 37, 154.
Surrender of Cornwallis, 146.
Surrender at Saratoga, 146.
Surrogate of New York, 144.
Surveyor-General, 69, 163.
Swartwout, Robert, 142.
Swartwout, Samuel, 9, 92, 142, 172.
Sylla, 98.
Tallmadge, James, 74, 118, 164, 177.
Tammanies, 40.
Tammany Hall, 41, 88, 112, 122, 140, 143, 155, 173, 177.
Tammany Society, 140, 152, 154, 155, 173, 177.
Tappan Sea, 84.
Targee, John, 2, 6, 34, 102, 122, 123, 173.
Tarquin, 71.
Tarrytown, 178.
Tartar Dogs, 23.
Taylor, General, 173.
Tea Party, 110.
Tea Room, 140.

Teazle, Sir Peter, 153.
Tennant, 48.
Tennessee, 166.
Thames Street, 174.
Thebes, 105.
Thomas, Simon, 157.
Thorburn, Grant, 57, 158, 159.
Thespian Fire, 73.
Titian, 14.
Toast, Gen. Jackson's, 2.
Tom Codus, 23.
Tom Thumb, 76.
Tompkins, Daniel D., 38, 154, 176.
Toraldi, Baron, 36.
Townsend, Peter I., 171.
Tract House, 155.
Tradesmen's Bank, 99.
Treasurer, State, 163.
Trinity Church, 175.
Tripper, Mr., 159.
Trumbull, Col. John, 14, 15, 146, 178.
Trumbull, Gov. Jonathan, 146.
Tully, 71, 163.
Turkish Wives, 64.
Tyber's Wave, 62.
Tyler, President, 175.
Tyrolese Airs, 162.
Ulster County, 141, 144, 165.
Ulysses, 71, 163.
United States Bank, 161.
United States Congress, 143, 166.
United States Consul, 137.
United States Supreme Court, 138.
Upham, 25.
Utica, 143.
Van Buren, Martin, 74, 80, 85, 99, 168, 172.
Vandervoort & Flandin, 83, 168.
Van Rensselaer, Gen. Stephen, 142.
Van Wyck, Pierre, 76, 89, 120, 122, 165, 171.
Varick Street, 153.
Verges, 75.
Vera Cruz, 139.
Verplanck, Gulian C., 152.
Virgil, 163.
Virginia, 30.
Von Hoffman, Baron, 162.
Vortex, 76.
Vosburgh, Abraham, 166.
Wall Street, 114, 148, 157, 161, 167.
Wallack, James W., 128, 138, 157, 179.

INDEX.

Wallack's Theatre, 179.
Ward, 133.
Warner, 75, 89, 165.
Warner, Col. Everardus, 40, 155, 171.
Warner, James, 171.
Washington, 119, 146, 154.
Washington Benevolent Society, 147.
Washington County, 165, 172.
Washington Hall, 142, 147.
Watts's Psalms and Hymns, 159.
Weeks, Capt. Seaman, Address to, 40.
Wehawk Hill, 66.
Wehawken, 172.
Wendover, Peter H., 76, 166.
West, Benj., 125, 126.
Whispering Post, 178.
White, Bishop, 175.
Whitehall, 99.
Wignell, 164.

Wigwam, Tammany, 155.
Willard, Mr., 161.
William Street, 156.
Williams Caleb, 174.
Windermere, 47.
Witch of Endor, 125.
Witches, 75.
Wood, 153.
Woodworth, 25, 74.
Woodworth, John, 164.
Woodworth, Samuel, 12, 144, 145, 168.
Wordsworth, 47.
Working Men, Epistle to Chairman of Committee of, 104.
Wortman, Tennis, 80, 168.
Wright, Frances, 138.
Yale College, 70.
Yates, 119.
Yonkers, 173.
York Theatre, 150.
Young, William, 158, 159.

www.ingramcontent.com/pod-product-compliance
Lightning Source LLC
Chambersburg PA
CBHW020913230426
43666CB00008B/1433